ELEMENTS

OF

POLITICAL ECONOMY,

BY

JAMES MILL, ESQ.

Scientia propter potentiam; Theorema propter problemata; omnis denique speculatio, actionis vel operis alicujus gratiâ, instituta est.

HOBBES.

THIRD EDITION,

REVISED AND CORRECTED.

LONDON:

PRINTED FOR BALDWIN, CRADOCK, AND JOY.

1826.

C. Baldwin, Printer,
New Bridge-street, London.

PREFACE.

THERE are few things of which I have occasion to advertize the reader, before he enters upon the perusal of the following work.

My object has been to compose a school-book of Political Economy, to detach the essential principles of the science from all extraneous topics, to state the propositions clearly and in their logical order, and to subjoin its demonstration to each. I am, myself, persuaded, that nothing more is necessary for understanding every part of the book, than to read it with attention ; such attention as persons of either sex, of ordinary understanding, are capable of bestowing.

They who are commencing the study ought to proceed slowly, and to familiarize themselves with the new combinations of ideas, as they are successively presented to them. If they proceed to a subsequent proposition before they are sufficiently imbued with the first, they will of course experience a difficulty, only because they have not present to their memory the truth which is calculated to remove it. If they who begin the study of mathematics were to content themselves with merely reading and assenting to the demonstrations, they would soon arrive at doctrines, which they would be unable to comprehend, solely because they had not, by frequent repetition, established in their minds those previous propositions, on which the evidence of the subsequent ones depends.

In a work of this description I have thought it adviseable not to quote any authorities, because I am anxious that the learner should fix his mind upon the doctrine and its evidence, without any extraneous consideration. I cannot fear an imputation of plagiarism, because I profess to have made no discovery; and those men who have contributed to the progress of the science need no testimony of mine to establish their fame.

————————

In this third edition, the only alterations, not merely verbal, will be found, in the section on Profits, where the different modes of expressing the relation of profits to wages is more fully expounded; in the section which treats of " what determines the quantity in which commodities exchange for one another," where I have added something in illustration of the analysis of what regulates value; in the section, which explains the " occasions on which it is the interest of nations to exchange commodities with one another," where I have corrected an error of the former editions; and in the section, which treats of a tax per acre on the land, where I have thought it necessary to explain a case to which I had not before adverted.

CONTENTS.

CHAPTER III.

ELEMENTS

OF

POLITICAL ECONOMY.

INTRODUCTION.

THE SUBJECT—ITS LIMITS—AND DIVISION.

POLITICAL ECONOMY is to the State, what domestic economy is to the family.

The family consumes; and, in order to consume, it must supply.

Domestic economy has, therefore, two grand objects; the consumption and supply of the family. The consumption being a quantity always indefinite, for there is no end to the desire of enjoyment, the grand concern is, to increase the supply.

B

Those things, which are produced, in sufficient abundance for the satisfaction of all, without the intervention of human labour; as air, the light of the sun, water, and so on; are not objects of care or providence; and therefore, accurately speaking, do not form part of the subject of domestic economy. The art of him, who manages a family, consists in regulating the supply and consumption of those things, which cannot be obtained but with cost; in other words, with human labour, " the original purchase-money, which is given for every thing."

The same is the case with Political Economy. It also has two grand objects, the Consumption of the Community, and that Supply upon which the consumption depends. Those things, which are supplied without the intervention of human labour, as nothing is required in order to obtain them, need not be taken into account. Had every thing, desired for consumption, existed without human labour, there would have been no place for Political Economy. Science is not implied in putting forth the hand, and using. But when labour is to be employed, and the objects of desire can be multiplied only by a preconcerted plan of operations, it becomes an object of importance to ascertain completely the means of that multiplication, and to frame a system of rules for applying them with greatest advantage to the end.

It is not pretended, that writers on Political Economy have always limited their disquisitions to this object. It seems, however, important to detach the science from all considerations not essential to it. The Reader is therefore requested to observe that, in the following pages, I have it merely in view, to ascertain the laws, according to which the production and consumption are regulated of those commodities, which the intervention of human labour is necessary to procure.

The Science of Political Economy, thus defined, divides itself into two grand inquiries ; that which relates to Production, and that which relates to Consumption.

But, after things are produced, it is evident, that, before they are consumed, they must be distributed. The laws of distribution, therefore, constitute an intermediate inquiry.

When commodities are produced, and distributed, it is highly convenient, for the sake both of reproduction and consumption, that portions of them should be exchanged for one another. To ascertain, therefore, the laws, according to which commodities are exchanged for one another, is a second inquiry, preceding that which relates to the last great topic of Political Economy, Consumption.

It thus appears, that four inquiries are comprehended in this science.

1st. What are the laws, which regulate the production of commodities :

2dly. What are the laws, according to which the commodities, produced by the labour of the community, are distributed :

3dly. What are the laws, according to which commodities are exchanged for one another :

4thly. What are the laws, which regulate consumption.

CHAPTER I.

PRODUCTION.

THE distinction, between what is done by labour, and what is done by nature, is not always observed.

Labour produces its effects only by conspiring with the laws of nature.

It is found that the agency of man can be traced to very simple elements. He does nothing but produce motion. He can move things towards one another, and he can separate them from one another.

The properties of matter perform the rest. He moves ignited iron to a portion of gunpowder, and an explosion takes place. He moves the seed to the ground, and vegetation commences. He separates the plant from the ground, and vegetation ceases. Why, or how, these effects take place, he is ignorant. He has only ascertained, by experience, that if he perform such and such motions, such and such events are the consequence. In strictness of speech, it is matter itself, which produces the effects. All that men can do is to place the objects of nature in a certain position. The tailor, when he makes a coat; the farmer, when he produces corn, do but the same thing. Each performs a set of motions; the properties of matter accomplish the rest. It would be absurd to ask, to which of any two effects the properties of matter contribute the most; seeing they contribute every thing, after certain portions of matter are placed in a certain position.

As our inquiry is confined to that species of production, of which human labour is the instrument; and as human labour produces its effects chiefly in two modes; either with, or without, the aid of implements; this chapter naturally divides itself into two sections; of which the first will treat of Labour, simply, and as much as possible detached from the consideration of the instruments by which the powers of labour may be improved : the second will treat of Capital, or of the origin, and nature of that provision of materials, on which labour is employed, and by which its operations are assisted.

SECTION I.

LABOUR.

In the state of society, in which we exist, we seldom see Labour employed except in conjunction with Capital. To conceive the separate operation of Labour more distinctly, it may be useful to recur, in imagination, to that simple state of things, in which society may be conceived to have originated.

When the savage climbs a tree, and gathers the fruit; when he ensnares a wild beast, or beats it down with a club, he may be considered as operating with his naked powers, and without the aid of any thing, to which the name of Capital can properly be annexed.

The principal thing, which, with a view to the conclusions of Political Economy, it is necessary to remark, in regard to Labour, considered as a distinct portion of a composite whole, and apart from Capital, is, the necessity of subsistence to the labourer. In the idea of labour, the idea of this subsistence is included. Whenever we say that such and such effects are produced by pure labour, we mean the consumption and operations of the labourer, taken conjunctly. There can be no labour, without the consumption of the labourer. If the man, who climbs the tree to gather the fruit, can manage to find two such trees, and to climb them in a day, he can continue his employment with the subsistence of half a day provided in advance. If the man who subsists on animals cannot make sure of his prey, in less than a day, he cannot have less than a whole day's subsistence in advance. If hunting excursions are undertaken, which occupy a week or a month, subsistence for several days may be required. It is evident, when men come to live upon those productions which their labour raises from the soil, and which can be brought to maturity only once in the year, that subsistence for a whole year must be laid up in advance.

The previous provision of the labourer may be greater or smaller, in different cases, in proportion to the greater or less time, which it may require, to realize the fruit of his labour, in the shape of subsistence; but in all these cases, equally, whenever we speak of his labour, as a thing by itself, a detached, independent, instrument of production, the idea of the subsistence is included in it.

This is the more necessary to be remembered, that the terms, Labour, and Wages, are, sometimes, incautiously used ; and confusion of ideas, and some fundamental errors, are the consequence. It is clear, that, when we speak of the labour of a man, for a day, or a month, or a year, the idea of his subsist-ence is as necessarily included, as that of the action of his muscles, or his life. His labour is not one thing, the action of his muscles another thing ; to the purpose in hand, they are one and the same thing. If wages be taken as synonymous with the con-sumption of the labourer, the labour cannot be taken, as one item of an aggregate, and its wages as an-other. As often as this is done, an error is the necessary consequence.

Having thus seen, what ideas are necessarily in-cluded in that of labour, in its detached, and simplest form, it is only further necessary, under this head, to consider the improvements, in respect to its pro-ductive powers, of which it is susceptible.

It will be seen hereafter, that the most important of these improvements arise, from the use of those instruments, which form one of the portions of ca-pital. Great improvements also arise, from the divi-sion, including the distribution, of labour.

The foundation of this latter class of improve-ments is laid, in the fact, that an operation, which we perform slowly at first, is performed with greater and greater rapidity by repetition. This is a law of human nature so familiar, and well understood, that it hardly stands in need of illustration. The simplest of all operations, that of beating a drum, is a proper example. A man who has not practised this operation, is often surprised, upon trial, at the slowness with which he performs it, while the rapidity of a practised drummer is still more astonishing.

The repetition, upon which the greatest celerity depends, must be frequent. It is not therefore compatible with a great number of different operations. The man, who would perform one, or a few, operations, with the greatest possible rapidity, must confine himself to one or a few. Of the operations, therefore, conducive to the production of the commodities desired by man, if any one confines himself to a small number, he will perform them with much more rapidity, than if he employed himself in a greater; and not only with more rapidity, but, what is often of the highest consequence, with greater correctness and precision.

A certain immense aggregate of operations, is subservient to the production of the commodities useful and agreeable to man. It is of the highest importance that this aggregate should be divided into portions, consisting, each, of as small a number of operations as possible, in order that every operation may be the more quickly and perfectly performed. If each man could, by the more frequent repetition thus occasioned, perform two of these operations, instead of one, and also perform each of them better, the powers of the community, in producing articles useful and agreeable to them, would, upon this supposition, be more than doubled. Not only would they be doubled in quantity, but a great advantage would be gained in point of quality.

This subject has been fully illustrated by Dr. Smith, in the first chapter of the first book of the " Inquiry into the Nature and Causes of the Wealth of Nations," where the extraordinary effect of the division of labour in increasing its productive powers, in the more complicated cases, is displayed in some very remarkable instances. He states that a boy, who has been accustomed to make nothing but nails, can make upwards of two thousand three hundred in a day; while a common blacksmith, whose operations are nevertheless so much akin to those of the nailer, cannot make above three hundred, and those very bad ones.

Even in the simplest state of labour, it cannot be doubted, that, if one man should confine himself to the operation of climbing trees for their fruit, another to the operations of ensnaring and killing animals, they would acquire a dexterity, the one in climbing trees, the other in procuring animals, greater than they would have acquired, had each occasionally performed both operations; and that they would by such means obtain a greater abundance, both of fruit, and of game.

So obvious is this advantage, that some remarkable cases of the division of labour are exemplified, in the earliest stages of the arts. The hands which spin the thread, and the hands which weave it into cloth, were different, in every country, perhaps, in which we have any memorial of the early state of the art. The man who tans the hide, and the man who makes it into shoes; the man who works in iron, and the man who works in wood, were all separated at an early period, and had divisions of labour appropriated to them.

If the immense aggregate of the operations which are subservient to the complicated accommodations, required in an artificial and opulent state of society, were to be divided, under circumstances the best calculated for breaking it down into those small groupes of operations, which afford the greatest aid to the productive powers of labour, the most perfect philosophical analysis of the subject would be the first operation to be performed; the next would be an equally perfect philosophical synthesis.

In order to know what is to be done with a vast aggregate of materials, existing in forms, ill adapted to the ends which are to be obtained, it is necessary to contemplate the aggregate in its elements; to resolve it into those elements; and carefully and comprehensively to pass them under review. This is the analytical operation.

When we have the full knowledge of the elements, which we are to combine, as means, towards our ends, and when we have an equally perfect knowledge of the ends, it then remains that we proceed to form those combinations, by which the ends will be most advantageously produced. This is the synthetical operation.

It is well known, that neither of these operations has as yet been performed, in order to obtain the best division and distribution of labour. It is equally certain, that this division is still in a most imperfect state. As far as it has been performed, it has been performed practically, as they call it; that is, in a great degree, accidentally; as the fortuitous discoveries of individuals, engaged in particular branches, enabled them to perceive that in these branches a particular advantage was to be gained. Such improvements have almost always been founded on some very narrow view; an analysis and synthesis, certainly; but including a small number of elements, and these but imperfectly understood. Improvements, founded upon narrow views, are almost always equally confined in their application. There is no generalization. An improvement, introduced into one machine, or one manufacture, is often long before it is introduced into another, where it would be equally important. And one improvement is still more slow in suggesting another, which is akin to it; because a narrow view discovers no relations, between the things which it embraces, and the things which it excludes.

SECTION II.

CAPITAL.

WE have already observed, that labour performs its operations, either simply, by the unaided powers of the human body ; or, with the use of instruments, which augment not only the quantity, but often also the accuracy and precision of its results.

As examples of the earliest and simplest of the instruments, contrived for this purpose, we may mention the bow and arrow, and the sling, of the huntsman. The spade is an instrument easily invented for turning the soil; and a certain rude machine, to which the force of cattle may be applied, and which is the first form of a plough, suggests itself at an early stage of improvement.

From these beginnings men proceed, inventing one instrument after another, the axe, the hammer, the saw, the wheel, the wheel-carriage, and so on, till they arrive at last at that copious supply of complicated machinery by which labour is rendered productive in the most artificial states of society. The provision which is made of these instruments is denominated capital.

This, however, is not the whole of what is denominated capital. Labour in its earliest stage is not employed upon any materials but such as nature presents, without any preparation at the hands of man. When the savage climbs the tree, to gather the fruit; when the huntsman tears down the branch, to form his club or his bow, he operates upon materials, which are prepared for him by the hand of nature. At a subsequent stage in the progress of industry, the materials upon which labour is employed, have generally been the result of previous labour. Thus, the flax and the cotton, which are to be manufactured into cloth and muslin, have been the result of the labour of agriculture; the iron has been the result of the labours of the miner and smelter, and so of other things. The materials, upon which labour is to be employed, when they have thus been the result of previous labour, are also denominated capital.

When we speak of labour, as one of the instruments of production, and of capital, as the other, these two constituents, namely, the instruments which aid labour, and the materials on which it is employed, are all that can be correctly included in the idea of capital. It is true that wages are in general included under that term. But, in that sense, labour is also included; and can no longer be spoken of as an instrument of production apart from capital.

C

We have already seen, that, whenever labour is spoken of as a separate, distinct, instrument of production, the idea of the subsistence, or consumption, of the labourer, for which wages is but another name, is included in the idea of the labour.

Having thus endeavoured to annex precise ideas to the terms Capital and Labour, a matter of the utmost importance in the study of political economy, and to distinguish their respective departments, in the business of production, it is only further necessary, to advert to the origin of capital, and the laws of its accumulation.

It is easy to discover, that the source, from which capital is ultimately derived, is labour. Production, of necessity, begins with the hands. There can be no instrument till it is made; and the first instrument had no previous instrument to be made with.

The first portion of capital, therefore, was the result of pure labour, without the co-operation of capital.

Speedily, however, after the first instrument, which increased the productive powers of labour, had been made, another instrument would be made to assist in the formation of it, as a knife, to aid in the formation of the bow; and then capital, for the first time, becomes the result of labour, and of capital, conjoined.

This subject is too clear to need to be illustrated, by tracing the mode, in which capital and labour combine, in producing the articles, of which capital is composed, from the simplest, to the most complicated, cases. It will be hereafter seen, that, in the more artificial and improved states of the business of production, a very great proportion of the whole of the labour and capital of the country is constantly employed in the production of the articles, which form capital.

As capital, from its simplest, to its most complicated state, means, something produced, for the purpose of being employed, as the means towards a further production; it is evidently a result of what is called saving.

Without saving there could be no capital. If all labour were employed upon objects of immediate consumption, all immediately consumed, such as the fruit, for which the savage climbs the tree, no article of capital, no article to be employed, as a means to further production, would ever exist. To this end, something must be produced, which is not immediately consumed; which is saved and set apart for another purpose.

Of the consequences of this fact, all, to which it is necessary here to advert, are sufficiently obvious.

Every article, which is thus saved, becomes an article of capital. The augmentation of capital, therefore, is every where exactly in proportion to the degree of saving; in fact, the amount of that augmentation, annually, is the same thing with the amount of the savings, which are annually made.

The labour and the capital, which combine to the production of a commodity, may belong both to one party, or one of them may belong to one party, the other to another. Thus, when the savage, who kills a deer, kills it with his own bow and arrows, he is the owner both of the labour and of the capital: when he kills it with the bow and arrows of another man, the one is the owner of the labour, the other of the capital. The man, who cultivates his little farm with his own labour and that of his family, without the aid of hired servants, is owner both of the capital and of the labour. The man, who cultivates with none but hired servants, is owner of the capital. The servants may be considered, at least for the present purpose, as owners of the labour, though we shall presently see under what modification that meaning is to be taken.

In this sense of the term " owners of labour," the parties, concerned about production, are divided into two classes, that of capitalists, the rich men who supply the materials and instruments of production ; and that of the workmen, who supply the labour.

These terms are all sufficiently familiar; but a few observations are further necessary, in order, on this important subject, to preclude, as far as possible, confusion of ideas.

The great capitalist, the owner of a manufactory, if he operated with slaves instead of free labourers, like the West India planter, would be regarded as owner both of the capital, and of the labour. He would be owner, in short, of both instruments of production : and the whole of the produce, without participation, would be his own.

What is the difference, in the case of the man, who operates by means of labourers receiving wages? The labourer, who receives wages, sells his labour for a day, a week, a month, or a year, as the case may be. The manufacturer, who pays these wages, buys the labour, for the day, the year, or whatever period it may be. He is equally therefore the owner of the labour, with the manufacturer who operates with slaves. The only difference is, in the mode of purchasing. The owner of the slave purchases, at once, the whole of the labour, which the man can ever perform : he, who pays wages, purchases only so much of a man's labour as he can perform in a day, or any other stipulated time. Being equally, however, the owner of the labour, so purchased, as the owner of the slave is of that of the slave, the produce, which is the result of this labour, combined with his capital, is all equally his own. In the state of society, in which we at present exist, it is in these circumstances that almost all production is effected : the capitalist is the owner of both instruments of production : and the whole of the produce is his.

There is a distinction of capital into two sorts, arising from a difference in the mode of applying it. To this distinction as some consequences of importance are attached, it is necessary that a correct idea should be attained of it.

Of the articles, whereof capital consists, some are of a durable nature, and contribute to production without being destroyed. Of this nature is a great proportion of the tools and machines, which are employed both in agriculture and manufactures. Such are the buildings subservient to the various kinds of production; and such are all the other accommodations, not necessary to be enumerated, which do not perish in the using. That portion of capital, which comes under this description, has been denominated " Fixed Capital."

There is another portion of the articles, subservient to production, which do perish in the using. Such are all the tools worn out in one set of operations, all the articles, which contribute to production only by their consumption, as coals, oil, the dye stuffs of the dyer, the seed of the farmer, and so on. Of this nature, also, are the raw materials worked up in the finished manufacture. The wool of the clothier is consumed in the making of his cloth, the cotton of the cotton-manufacturer in making his muslins. Under the same head must be included the expence of repairing and keeping in order the more durable articles of fixed capital. The distinctive character of all this portion of capital is, that it is necessarily consumed, in contributing to production, and that it must be reproduced, in order to enable the producer to continue his operations. This has been denominated " circulating " capital ; but by a very inappropriate appellation. There is nothing in its consumption and reproduction which bears much resemblance to circulation. It would be much better to call it " reproduced " capital, although the word " reproduced," being a past and not a future participle, is not unexceptionable ; it is capital which constantly needs to be reproduced, because, in contributing to production, it is constantly consumed.

There is another thing, which is also constantly consumed, and constantly needs to be reproduced, and that is, the subsistence, or consumption, or wages of the labourer; and that, equally, whether the labourer supplies it to himself, or receives it from the capitalist, in the shape of wages; that is, pay, in advance, for his labour. In this latter shape, being advanced by the capitalist out of those funds, which would otherwise have constituted capital in the distinctive sense of the word, and being considered as yielding the same advantage, it is uniformly spoken of under the name of capital, and a confusion of ideas is sometimes the consequence.

When all these items are included, it is obvious, that a very great proportion of the consumption and production, of every country, takes place for the sake of reproduction. This is a highly important fact, of which the consequences will hereafter occur for more particular consideration.

It follows, necessarily, if the instruments of labour, the materials on which it is employed, and the subsistence of the labourer, are all included under the name of capital, that the productive industry of every country is in proportion to its capital; increases when its capital increases; and declines when it declines. If the instruments of labour, the materials to work upon, and the pay of workmen, are all increased, the quantity of work will be increased, provided more workmen can be obtained. If more workmen cannot be obtained, two things will happen: First, wages will be raised; which, giving an impulse to population, will increase the number of labourers: Secondly, the scarcity of hands will whet the ingenuity of capitalists to supply the deficiency, by new inventions in machinery, and by distributing and dividing labour to greater advantage.

CHAPTER II.

DISTRIBUTION.

WE have seen that two classes of persons are concerned in production; Labourers, and Capitalists. Each of these classes must have its share of the commodities produced: or, which comes to the same thing, of the benefit derived from them. When the Land is one of the instruments of production, another party comes in for a portion; I mean, the Owners of the Land. And these three classes; the labourers, the capitalists, and the landlords; immediately share, that is, divide among them, the whole of the annual produce of the country.

When the parties are determined, among whom the whole of the produce is distributed, it remains to be ascertained, by what laws the proportions are established, according to which the division is made. We shall begin with the explanation of Rent, or the share received by Landlords; as it is the most simple, and will facilitate the explanation of the laws, upon which the shares, of the Labourers, and of the Capitalists, depend.

SECTION I.

RENT.

LAND is of different degrees of fertility. There is a species of land, the elevated or stony parts, for example, of high mountains, loose sand, and certain marshes, which may be said to produce nothing. Between this and the most productive sort, there are lands of all the intermediate degrees of fertility.

Again ; lands, of the highest fertility, do not yield the whole of what they are capable of yielding, with the same facility. A piece of land, for example, may be capable of yielding annually ten quarters of corn, or twice ten, or three times ten. It yields, however, the first ten, with a certain quantity of labour, the second ten, not without a greater, the third ten, not without a greater still, and so on ; every additional ten requiring to its production a greater cost than the ten which preceded it. This is well known to be the law, according to which, by a greater expenditure of capital, a greater produce is obtained, from the same portion of land.

Till the whole of the best land is brought under cultivation, and till it has received the application of a certain quantity of capital, all the capital employed upon the land is employed with an equal return. At a certain point, however, no additional capital can be employed upon the same land, without a diminution of return. In any country, therefore, after a certain quantity of corn has been raised, no greater quantity can be raised, but at a greater cost. If such additional quantity is raised, the capital, employed upon the land, may be distinguished into two portions ; one, producing a higher ; another, a lower return.

When capital producing a lower return is applied to the land, it is applied in one of two ways. It is either applied to new land of the second degree of fertility, then for the first time brought under culti-vation ; or it is applied to land of the first degree of fertility, which has already received all the capital which can be applied without a diminution of return.

Whether capital shall be applied to land of the second degree of fertility, or in a second dose to the land of the first degree of fertility, will depend, in each instance, upon the nature and qualities of the two soils. If the same capital which will produce only eight quarters, when applied in a second dose to the best land, will produce nine quarters, when applied to land of the second degree of fertility, it will be applied to that land, and *vice versâ*.

The land of the different degrees of fertility ; first, or highest sort ; second, or next highest, and so on, may, for facility of reference, be denominated, No. 1, No. 2, No. 3, &c. In like manner, the different doses of capital, which may be applied to the same land, one after another, with less and less effect, may be denominated 1st dose, 2d dose, 3d dose, and so on.

So long as land produces nothing, it is not worth appropriating. So long as a part only of the best land is required for cultivation, all that is uncultivated yields nothing; that is, nothing which has any value. It naturally, therefore, remains unappropriated; and any man may have it, who undertakes to render it productive.

During this time, land, speaking correctly, yields no rent. There is a difference, no doubt, between the land which has been cultivated, and the land which is yet uncleared for cultivation. Rather than clear the fresh land, a man will pay an equivalent, annual, or otherwise, for the cost of clearing: and it is evident that he will pay no more. This, therefore, is not a payment for the power of the soil, but simply for the capital bestowed upon the soil. It is not rent; it is interest.

The time, however, arrives, as population, and the demand for food increase, when it is necessary either to have recourse to land of the second quality, or to apply a second dose of capital, less productively, upon land of the first quality.

If a man cultivates land of the second quality, upon which a certain quantity of capital will produce only eight quarters of corn, while the same quantity of capital upon land of the first quality will produce ten quarters; it will make no difference to him, whether he pay two quarters for leave to cultivate the first sort, or cultivate the second without any payment. He will therefore be content to pay two quarters for leave to cultivate the first sort; and that payment constitutes rent.

Let us suppose, again, that instead of cultivating land of the second quality, it is more advisable to apply a second dose of capital to land of the first quality; and that, while the first dose produces ten quarters, the second, of equal amount, will produce only eight quarters; it is equally implied in this, as in the former case, that it is impossible to employ any more capital with so great an effect as the ten supposed quarters, and that there are persons who are willing to apply it with so little a return as eight. But if there are persons who are willing to apply their capital on the land with so little a return as eight quarters, the owners of the land may make a bargain, by which they will obtain all that is produced above eight. The effect upon rent is thus the same in both cases.

It follows that rent increases in proportion as the productive power of the capital, successively bestowed upon the land, decreases. If population has arrived at another stage, when, all the land of second quality being cultivated, it is necessary to have recourse to land of third quality, yielding, instead of eight quarters, only six, it is evident, from the same process of reasoning, that the land of second quality will now yield rent, namely, two quarters; and that land of first quality will yield an augmented rent, namely, two quarters more. The case will be exactly the same, if, instead of having recourse to land of less fertility, a second and a third dose of capital, with the same diminution of produce, are bestowed upon land of the first quality.

We may thus obtain a general expression for rent. In applying capital, either to lands of various degrees of fertility, or, in successive doses, to the same land, some portions of the capital so employed are attended with a greater produce, some with a less. That which yields the least, yields all that is necessary for re-imbursing and rewarding the capitalist. The capitalist will receive no more than this remuneration for any portion of the capital which he employs, because the competition of others will prevent him. All that is yielded above this remuneration, the landlord will be able to appropriate. Rent, therefore, is the difference between the return made to the more productive portions, and that which is made to the least productive portion, of capital, employed upon the land.

D

Taking, for illustration, the three cases, of ten quarters, eight quarters, and six quarters, we perceive, that rent is the difference between six quarters and eight quarters for the portion of capital which yields only eight quarters; the difference between six quarters and ten quarters for the portion of capital which yields ten quarters; and if three doses of capital, one yielding ten, another eight, and another six quarters, are applied to the same portion of land, its rent will be four quarters for dose No. 1, and two quarters for dose No. 2, making together six quarters for the whole.

If these conclusions are well supported, the doctrine of rent is simple, and the consequences, as we shall see hereafter, are exceedingly important. There is but one objection, which it seems possible to make to them. It may be said, that, after land is appropriated, there is no portion of it which does not pay rent, no owner being disposed to give the use of it for nothing. This objection has, indeed, been raised; and it has been urged, that some rent is paid even for the most barren of the Scottish mountains.

If an objection is taken, it affects the conclusion, either to a material, or to an immaterial extent. Where the matter alleged in objection, even if admitted, would still leave the conclusion substantially, and to all practical purposes, true, the objection must be owing to one of two defects in the mind of the objector; either a confusion of ideas, which prevents him from seeing to how small a degree the matter which he alleges affects the doctrine which he denies; or a disposition to evade the admission of the doctrine, even though nothing solid can be found with which to oppose it.

That the matter alledged in this objection, even if allowed, would leave the conclusion, to all practical purposes, just where it was, can hardly fail to be acknowledged, as soon as the circumstances are disclosed. It cannot be so much as pretended that the rent paid for the barren mountains of Scotland is any thing but a trifle; an evanescent quantity, when we speak of any moderate extent. If it were 5*l.* for a thousand acres, that is, about one penny per acre, it would bear so small a proportion to the cost of cultivation, which could not be less than several pounds per acre, that it would little affect the truth of the conclusion we have endeavoured to establish.

Let us suppose, for the sake of the argument, that the worst species of land under cultivation pays one penny per acre: rent, in that case, would be the difference between the produce resulting from different portions of capital, as explained above, with the correction required on account of the penny per acre paid as rent for the worst species of land under cultivation. Assuredly, if right in every other respect, we shall not be far wrong in our conclusions, by leaving this penny out of the question. A very slight advantage, in simplifying our language on the subject, would justify this omission.

But it is not true, that our conclusions stand in need of any such correction, even for metaphysical exactness. There is land, such as the sands of Arabia, which yields nothing. Land is found at all the intermediate stages from this to the highest fertility. Some land, though not absolutely incapable of yielding any thing for the accommodation of man, could not be made to yield what would maintain the labourers required for its cultivation. This land can never be cultivated. There is land, the annual produce of which would just maintain the labour necessary for its cultivation, and no more. This land is just capable of being cultivated, but obviously incapable of paying rent. The objection, therefore, is not only practically immaterial, it is metaphysically unsound.

It may be safely affirmed, that there is no country, of any considerable extent, in which there is not land incapable of yielding rent : that is, incapable of yielding to human labour more than would be necessary for the maintenance of that labour. That such, at least, is the case in this country, seems very unlikely to be disputed. There are parts of its mountains where nothing less hardy than heath, others where nothing but moss, can vegetate. When it is asserted that every part of the mountains of Scotland pays rent, the state of the facts is misunderstood. It is only true that there is no tenant of any portion of any man's estate in the highlands of Scotland, who does not pay rent. The reason is, because even in the mountains of Scotland there are spots in the valleys, the produce of which is considerable. It does not follow, though hundreds of acres of mountain are added to these valleys, that therefore every part of the mountain yields rent; it is certain that many parts neither do nor can.

Even where the land is not absolutely barren, and where there is still something for the more hardy of the useful animals to pick up, it is not to be allowed that rent is the necessary consequence. It ought to be remembered, that these cattle are capital, and that the land must afford enough not only to make the return for that capital, but to pay for the tendance of the cattle, of which, in such situations, especially in winter, not a little is required. Unless the land yields all this, and something more, it cannot yield any rent.

In the greater part of this island, there is hardly a farm, of any considerable extent, which does not contain land, some of more, some of less fertility, varying from a high or moderate degree of fertility, down to land which yields not enough to afford any rent. Of course I do not request admission to this affirmation upon my authority ; I rest it upon an appeal to the experience of those men who are best acquainted with the circumstances. If the state of the facts corresponds with the affirmation, it follows demonstratively, that the last portion of the land which is placed under cultivation yields no rent. In such farms as those we have now described, the tenant has bargained for a certain sum to the landlord. That, of course, was calculated, upon the produce of the land which yielded not only the proper return for the capital with which it was cultivated, but something more. As the motive of the tenant to cultivate is wholly constituted by the proper return to his capital, if there is any portion of the barren land, included in his farm, which will just yield the profit of stock, and no more ; though it will not afford any thing for rent, it affords to him the adequate motive for cultivation. It can hardly be denied that, in the insensible degrees by which land declines from greater to less fertility, there will, in all considerable farms, be generally found a portion with this particular degree and no more.

The conclusion, however, may be established, by the clearest evidence, without regard to the question, whether all land pays or does not pay rent. On land which pays the highest rent, we have seen that capital, applied in successive doses, is not attended with equal results. The first dose yields more, possibly much more, than the return for the capital. The second also may yield more, and so on. The rent, if accurately calculated, will be equal to all that is rendered by those several doses, over and above the profits of stock. The cultivator, of course, applies all those several doses of capital on which he has agreed to pay rent. But immediately after them comes another dose, which though it yields nothing for rent, may fully yield the ordinary profits of stock. It is for the profits of stock, and them alone, that the farmer cultivates. As long, therefore, as capital applied to his farm will yield the ordinary profits of stock, he will apply capital, if he has it. I therefore conclude, with assurance, that in the natural state of things, in every agricultural country, one portion of the capital employed upon the land pays no rent; that rent, therefore, consists wholly, of that produce which is yielded by the more productive portions of capital, over and above a quantity equal to that which constitutes the return to the least productive portion, and which must be received, to afford his requisite profits, by the farmer.

SECTION II.

WAGES.

PRODUCTION is performed by labour. Labour, however, receives the raw material which it fashions, and the machinery by which it is aided, from capital, or more properly speaking, these articles are the capital.

The labourer is sometimes the owner of all the capital which his labour requires. The shoemaker or tailor has, sometimes, not only the tools with which he works, but also the leather or cloth upon which his labour is employed. In all cases of that description, the commodity is wholly the property of the man by whose labour it is prepared.

In the greater number of cases, however, especially in the more improved stages of society, the labourer is one person, the owner of the capital another. The labourer has neither raw material nor tools. These requisites are provided for him by the capitalist. For making this provision, the capitalist, of course, expects a reward. As the commodity, which was produced by the shoemaker, when the capital was his own, belonged wholly to himself, and constituted the whole of his reward, both as labourer and capitalist, so, in this case, the commodity belongs to the labourer and capitalist together. When prepared, the commodity, or the value of it, is to be shared between them. The reward to both must be derived from the commodity, and the reward of both makes up the whole of the commodity.

Instead, however, of waiting till the commodity is produced, and abiding all the delay and uncertainties of the market in which the value of it is realized, it has been found to suit much better the convenience of the labourers to receive their share in advance. The shape under which it has been found most convenient for all parties that they should receive it, is that of wages. When that share of the commodity, which belongs to the labourer, has been all received in the shape of wages, the commodity itself belongs to the capitalist, he having, in reality, bought the share of the labourer and paid for it in advance.

1. *That the rate of wages depends on the proportion between Population, and Employment, in other words, Capital.*

We come now to the question as to what determines the share of the labourer, or the proportion in which the commodity, or its worth, is divided between him and the capitalist. Whatever the share of the labourer, such is the rate of wages; and, *vice versâ,* whatever the rate of wages, such is the share of the commodity, or commodity's worth, which the labourer receives.

It is very evident, that the share of the two parties is the subject of a bargain between them; and if there is a bargain, it is not difficult to see on what the terms of the bargain must depend. All bargains, when made in freedom, are determined by competition, and the terms alter according to the state of supply and demand.

Let us begin by supposing that there is a certain number of capitalists, with a certain quantity of food, raw material, and instruments, or machinery; that there is also a certain number of labourers; and that the proportion, in which the commodities produced are divided between them, has fixed itself at some particular point.

Let us next suppose, that the labourers have increased in number one half, without any increase in the quantity of capital. There is the same quantity of the requisites for the employment of labour; that is, of food, tools, and material, as there was before; but for every 100 labourers there are now 150. There will be 50 men, therefore, in danger of being left out of employment. To prevent their being left out of employment they have but one resource; they must endeavour to supplant those who have forestalled the employment; that is, they must offer to work for a smaller reward. Wages, therefore, decline.

If we suppose, on the other hand, that the quantity of capital has increased, while the number of labourers remains the same, the effect will be reversed. The capitalists have a greater quantity than before of the means of employment; of capital, in short; from which they wish to derive advantage. To derive this advantage they must have more labourers. To obtain them, they also have but one resource, to offer higher wages. But the masters by whom the labourers are now employed are in the same predicament, and will of course offer higher to induce them to remain. This competition is unavoidable, and the necessary effect of it is a rise of wages.

It thus appears, that, if population increases, without an increase of capital, wages fall; and that, if capital increases, without an increase of population, wages rise. It is evident, also, that if both increase, but one faster than the other, the effect will be the same as if the one had not increased at all, and the other had made an increase equal to the difference. Suppose, for example, that population has increased one-eighth, and capital one-eighth; this is the same thing as if they had stood still, with regard to the effect upon labour. But suppose that, in addition to the above-mentioned one-eighth, population had increased another eighth, the effect, in that case, upon wages, would be the same as if capital had not increased at all, and population had increased one-eighth.

Universally, then, we may affirm, that, other things remaining the same, if the ratio which capital and population bear to one another remains the same, wages will remain the same; if the ratio which capital bears to population increases, wages will rise; if the ratio which population bears to capital increases, wages will fall.

From this law, clearly understood, it is easy to trace the circumstances which, in any country, determine the condition of the great body of the people. If that condition is easy and comfortable, all that is necessary to keep it so, is, to make capital increase as fast as population; or, on the other hand, to prevent population from increasing faster than capital. If that condition is not easy and comfortable, it can only be made so, by one of two methods; either by quickening the rate at which capital increases, or retarding the rate at which population increases; augmenting, in short, the ratio which the means of employing the people bear to the number of people.

If it were the natural tendency of capital to increase faster than population, there would be no difficulty in preserving a prosperous condition of the people. If, on the other hand, it were the natural tendency of population to increase faster than capital, the difficulty would be very great. There would be a perpetual tendency in wages to fall. The progressive fall of wages would produce a greater and a greater degree of poverty among the people, attended with its inevitable consequences, misery and vice. As poverty, and its consequent misery increased, mortality would also increase. Of a numerous family born, a certain number only, from want of the means of well-being, would be reared. By whatever proportion the population tended to increase faster than capital, such a proportion of those who were born would die : the ratio of increase in capital and population would then remain the same, and the fall of wages would proceed no farther.

That population has a tendency to increase faster, than, in most places, capital has actually increased, is proved, incontestably, by the condition of the population in most parts of the globe. In almost all countries, the condition of the great body of the people is poor and miserable. This would have been impossible, if capital had increased faster than population. In that case wages must have risen ; and high wages would have placed the labourer above the miseries of want.

This general misery of mankind is a fact, which

can be accounted for, upon one only of two suppositions : either that there is a natural tendency in
population to increase faster than capital, or that
capital has, by some means, been prevented from increasing so fast as it has a tendency to increase. This,
therefore, is an inquiry of the highest importance.

2. *Proof of the tendency of Population to increase*
rapidly.

The natural tendency of population to increase is
to be collected from two sets of circumstances ; the
physiological constitution of the female of the human
species ; and the statements respecting the rate of
increase in different countries.

The facts respecting the physiological constitution
of the human female are well ascertained, and are
indubitable grounds of conclusion. The statements
respecting the rate of increase in different countries will be found to be, either suppositions with
respect to matters of fact, upon the conformity of
which suppositions to any real matters of fact we
can have no assurance ; or statements of facts, of such
a nature, as prove nothing with regard to the points
in dispute.

That the possible rate of increase in the numbers
of mankind depends upon the constitution of the fe-

male, will not be disputed. The facts, which are fully ascertained in regard to the female of the human species, and the inferences which the sciences of physiology and comparative anatomy enable us to derive from the analogy of other animals, whose anatomy and physiology resemble those of the human species, afford the means of very satisfactory conclusions on this subject.

The females of those species of animals, whose period and mode of gestation are similar to those of the female of our own species, and which bring forth one at a birth, are capable, when placed in the most favourable circumstances, of a birth every year, from the time when the power of producing begins, till the time when it ends, omitting one year now and then, which, at the most, amounts to a very small proportion on the whole.

The suckling of the infant, in the case of the female of the human species, if continued more than three months, has a tendency to postpone the epoch of conception beyond the period of a year. This, it is to be observed, is the only physiological peculiarity which authorizes an inference of any difference in the frequency of the births in the case of the female of the human species, and in that of those other species to which we have referred.

To reason correctly, we should make an allowance

for that peculiarity. Let such ample allowance be made as will include all interruptions ; let us say that one birth in two years is natural to the female of the human species. In Europe, to which we may at present confine our observations, the period of child-bearing in women extends, from sixteen or seventeen, to forty-five, years of age. Let us make still more allowance, and say it extends only from twenty to forty years of age. In that period, at the allowance of two years to one birth, there is time for ten births, which may be regarded as not more than the number natural to the female of the human species.

Under favourable circumstances, the mortality among children is very small. Mortality among the children of very poor people is unavoidable, from want of the necessary means of health. Among the children of people in easy circumstances, who know and practise the rules for the preservation of health, the mortality is small; and there can be no doubt, that, under more skilful modes of managing the food, and clothing, the air, the exercise, and education of children, even this mortality would be greatly diminished.

We may conclude, therefore, that, in the most favourable circumstances, ten births are the measure of fecundity in the female of the human species ; and that of the children born a small proportion would die before the age of maturity. For occasional instances of barrenness, and for this small degree of mortality, let us make much more than the necessary allowance, a deduction of one-half; and say, That every human pair, united at an early age, commanding a full supply of things necessary for physical welfare, exempt from the necessity of oppressive labour, and sufficiently skilled to make the best use of their circumstances for preventing disease and mortality among themselves and their children, would, one with another, rear five children. If this is the case, it is needless to exhibit an accurate calculation, to show that population would double itself in some moderate portion of years. It is evident, at once, that it would double itself in a small number of years.

To meet a conclusion so well established as this, recourse has been had to certain tables, respecting population, and respecting births and deaths, in various countries. The reasoning from these tables evades the point in dispute. I know no tables which exhibit any thing, even if we give them, what they never deserve, credit for exactness, except the mere fact with regard to the state of increase. They show, or pretend to show, whether a certain population is increasing or not increasing; and, if increasing, at what rate. But, if it appeared, from such tables, that the population of every country in the world were stationary, no man, capable of reasoning, would infer, that the human race is incapable of increasing. Every body knows the fact, that in the greater number of countries, the population is stationary, or nearly so. But what does this prove, so long as we are not informed, by what causes it is prevented from increasing? We know well, that there are two causes, by which it may be prevented from increasing, how great soever its natural tendency to increase. The one is poverty; under which, let the number born be what it may, all but a certain number undergo a premature destruction. The other is prudence; by which either marriages are sparingly contracted, or care is taken that children, beyond a certain number, shall not be the fruit. It is useless to inform us, that there is little or no increase of population in certain countries, if we receive not, at the same time, accurate information of the degree in which poverty, or prudence, or other causes, operate to prevent it.

That population, therefore, has such a tendency to increase as would enable it to double itself in a small number of years, is a proposition resting on the strongest evidence, which nothing worth the name of evidence has been brought to controvert.

3. *Proof that capital has a less tendency than Population to increase rapidly.*

We come next to consider the tendency which capital may have to increase. If that should increase as fast as population, along with every labourer produced, the means of employment and subsistence would also be produced; and no degradation of the great body of the people would be the consequence.

Though it is found, where property is secure, that there is a considerable disposition in mankind to save; sufficient, where vast consumption is not made by the government, and where the difficulties of production are not very great, to make capital progressive; this disposition is still so weak, in almost all the situations in which human beings have ever been placed, as to make the increase of capital slow.

The annual produce is always distributed in such a manner, that, either the great body of the people are liberally provided with what is necessary for subsistence and enjoyment, when of course a smaller portion goes to swell the incomes of the rich; or, the great body of the people are reduced to mere necessaries, when there is naturally a class of people whose incomes are large. To one or other of these two cases the state of every community approximates.

1. In the case, in which there is a class reduced to necessaries, and a class of rich, it is evident that the first have not the means of saving. A class of rich men, in the middle of a class of poor, are not apt to save. The possession of a large fortune generally whets the appetite for immediate enjoyment. And the man who is already in possession of a fortune, yielding him all the enjoyments which fortune can command, has little inducement to save. In such a state of the social order, any rapid increase of capital is opposed by causes which are in general irresistible.

2. We are next to consider the state of the social order, in which a large share of the annual produce is distributed among the great body of the people. In that situation, neither the class which labours, nor that which is maintained without labouring, has any forcible motives to save.

When a man possesses, what we are now supposing possessed by the great body of the people, food, clothing, lodging, and all other things sufficient not only for comfortable, but pleasurable existence, he possesses the means of all the substantial enjoyments of human life. The rest is in a great measure fancy. There are two sets of men; one, in whom the reasoning power is strong, and who are able to resist a present pleasure for a greater one hereafter; another, in whom it is weak, and who can seldom resist the charm of immediate enjoyment. Of course, it is not in the latter class that the motive to save can be expected to prevail. The class, on the other hand, in whom reason is sufficiently strong to form a due estimate of pleasures, cannot fail to perceive that those which they can obtain by adding penny to penny, after all the rational desires are satisfied, are not equal to the pleasures which, in the circumstances we have supposed, they must relinquish to obtain them. Both the higher and the lower principles of our nature are in such circumstances opposed to accumulation. So far, as to the strength of the motive which, in the supposed circumstances, can operate upon the labouring class.

What remains of the annual produce, after the share of the labouring class is deducted, is either distributed in large portions among a small number of very rich men, or among a large number of men of moderate fortunes.

We have already examined the state of the motives to accumulate when fortunes are large; and have found that it never can be such as to produce very considerable effects. We have now to examine the state of the motives to accumulate, in a society, in which there is a great number of moderate fortunes, without the prevalence of large. In the way of physical enjoyment, these fortunes yield every thing which the largest fortunes can bestow. There are only two motives, therefore, which, in this situation, can counteract the strong tendency to immediate enjoyment: either the desire of a command over the sentiments of mankind; or the wish to make a provision for children.

The strength of the motive to command by riches the favourable sentiments of mankind will depend upon the effect they are calculated to produce. That is different, in different states of society. In the state of society, supposed in the present case, men are distributed into two classes: men of easy but moderate fortunes; and a well paid body of labourers and artisans.

The first class; men with fortunes equal to all the purposes not only of independence, and of physical enjoyment, but of taste and elegance, and who at the same time constitute the governing portion of society, giving the tone to its sentiments and amusements; are not in the situation of men whose imaginations are apt to be dazzled by the glare of superior riches. The persons belonging to the second, or labouring class, are cringing and servile, where the frown of the rich man is terrible, and his little favours important: but when they are placed in circumstances which impart the feeling of independence, and give them opportunity for the cultivation of their minds, they are little affected by the signs of wealth. This, therefore, is a state of society in which the possession of great riches gives little command over the sentiments of others, and cannot constitute a powerful motive for saving.

With respect to the provision for children, if a man feels no great desire to make a larger than the ordinary moderate fortune for himself, he feels as little desire at the least to make it for his children. The provision, which he desires to make for them, can only, therefore, be such as to place them in the same situation which is held by himself. He will be anxious to afford to them the same means for beginning life advantageously, as were afforded, or would have been desirable, to himself. To this extent the desire of making a provision for children might be expected to be very general, and it would ensure a certain moderate increase of capital. This may therefore be considered, as, perhaps, the most favourable state of society for accumulation; with the exception of those cases in which colonists, with all the knowledge and power of civilized life, are transported into a country uninhabited, or nearly so, and have the power of cultivating without limit the most productive species of land. These are coincidences so extraordinary, and so rare, that, in tracing the general laws of human society, it is only necessary to show that they are not forgotten.

These considerations seem to prove that more than moderate effects can rarely flow from the motives to accumulation. But the proof, that population has a tendency to increase faster than capital, does not depend upon this foundation, strong as it is. The tendency of population to increase, whatever it may be, is at any rate an equable tendency. At what rate soever it has increased at any one time, it may be expected to increase at an equal rate, if placed in equally favourable circumstances, at any other time. The case with capital is the reverse.

Whether, after land of superior quality has been exhausted, capital is applied to new land of inferior quality, or in successive doses with diminished returns upon the same land, the produce of it is continually diminishing in proportion to its increase. It the return to capital is, however, continually decreasing, the annual fund, from which savings are made, is continually diminishing. The difficulty of making savings is thus continually augmented, and at last they must totally cease.

It thus sufficiently appears, that there is a tendency in population to increase faster than capital. If this be established, it is of no consequence to the present purpose to inquire about the rapidity of the increase. How slow soever the increase of population, provided that of capital is still slower, wages will be reduced so low that a portion of the population will regularly die of want. Neither can this dreadful consequence be averted otherwise than by the use of means to prevent the increase of capital from falling short of that of population.

---

4. *That forcible means employed to make capital increase faster than its natural tendency would not produce desirable effects.*

There are two modes in which artificial means may be employed to make population and capital keep pace together : expedients may be sought, either to restrain the tendency of population to increase ; or to accelerate beyond its natural pace the increase of capital.

The principal means, by which legislatures have it in their power to alter the course of human actions, is by rewards and punishments. Neither is very applicable to the purpose of counteracting the tendency in the human species to multiply. Suppose a law were proposed for annexing penalties to the father and mother of a child, the circumstances of whom were inadequate to its maintenance ; it would not be easy to find a mode of punishing, which would be equal to the effect, without producing almost as much uneasiness in society as that which it would propose to remedy : neither would it be very possible to ascertain and define the state of circumstances which is, and that which is not, adequate to the maintenance of one, or two, or any other number of children. To apply rewards to the case of not having any children, in such a manner as to operate usefully upon the principle of population, would be still more difficult.

Legislation, in cases ill adapted to its direct, can sometimes produce considerable effects by its indirect operation ; as when a desire, which gratifies itself in a hurtful course of action, and cannot easily be counteracted by reward and punishment, is drawn to gratify itself in a less hurtful or an innocent direction. If legislatures have taken measures, as they very often have done, sometimes by direct, more frequently by indirect means, to stimulate the principle of population, such mischievous legislation may be corrected.

The powerful agency of the popular sanction might in this, as in other cases, be turned to great account. If an intense degree of disapprobation were directed upon the men, who, by their folly, involved themselves, through a great family, in poverty and dependence ; of approbation upon those who, by their self command, preserved themselves from this misery and degradation, much of this folly would unquestionably be prevented.

The result to be aimed at is, to secure to the great body of the people all the happiness which is capable of being derived from the matrimonial union, without the evils which a too rapid increase of their numbers involves. The progress of legislation, the improvement of the education of the people, and the decay of superstition, will, in time, it may be hoped, accomplish the difficult task of reconciling these important objects.

Such are the modes in which legislation can weaken the tendency in population to increase. It remains to inquire by what means it can strengthen the tendency in capital to increase. These are, also, direct and indirect. As the legislature, if skilful, has great power over the tastes of the community, it may contribute to render frugality fashionable, and expense disgraceful. The legislature may also produce that distribution of property which experience shows to be the most favourable to saving. Sumptuary laws have been adopted in several countries; but it is not easy to contrive sumptuary laws, the effect of which would be very considerable, without a minute and vexatious interference with the ordinary business of life.

There is certainly one course by which the legislature might produce considerable effects upon the accumulation of capital; because it might lay hold of any portion which it pleased of the net produce of the year, and convert it into capital. We have only, therefore, to inquire, in what manner this could be performed, and what effects it would produce.

The mode of taking whatever portion it might find expedient, is obvious and simple. An income tax, of the proper amount, would effectually answer the purpose.

The legislature might employ the capital, thus forcibly created, in one or other of two ways : it might lend it to be employed by others : or it might retain the employment in its own hands.

The simplest mode, perhaps, would be, to lend it to those manufacturers and capitalists who might apply for it, and could give security for the re-payment. The interest of what was thus laid out in one year might be employed as capital the next. Every annual portion would thus make compound interest, and, so long as interest remained pretty high, would double itself in a small number of years. If wages appeared likely to fall, a higher income tax would be required. If wages rose higher than seemed to be necessary for the most desirable condition of the labourer, the income tax might be reduced.

Without waiting to inquire, whether a machinery, capable of producing these effects, be or be not practicable, we may proceed to another considera-tion, which seems calculated to decide the merits of the scheme.

According to the progress above supposed, the increase of population would be rapid. The progress would also be rapid, in the application of capital to land of a worse and worse quality, or in doses attended with a less and less return.

In proportion as capital is attended with less and less of annual return, the owners of capital have less and less income. If the income from capital be continually diminished, in process of time none but the owners of large masses of capital will derive from it the means of existence. This is the extreme state of things to which the operation of the scheme, supposing it not impracticable, certainly tends.

It remains to inquire how far these effects are to be considered as good.

Let us suppose that the command of the labourer over the articles of his consumption remains unaltered. Those who do not subsist by the wages of labour, live either upon the produce of stock, or upon the rent of land. In the case supposed, the tendency is, to impoverish those who live upon the produce of stock; but to increase the rent of land. With the exception of the owners of land, all the rest of the community would be either labourers, or capitalists almost equally poor. As often as land were offered to sale, a great amount of capital would of course be given for it; nobody, therefore, would be able to buy more than a very limited portion.

In this state of things, sales of land would either be frequent, or they would be rare. It is necessary to consider what would be the effects in either case.

The effects which would arise in the case in which the sales of land would be rare, are simple. The owners of land would be a comparatively small number of rich people, in the midst of a population, all equally, and hopelessly, poor. That there is scarcely any state of society less conducive to human happiness, we need not here spend any time to prove.

If sales went on, it being the nature of land, as of other property, to change hands continually, the whole land would be divided, at last, into very small portions; covered by a dense population, no portion of whom would be in circumstances much better than those of the labourer. Is this, in itself, a desirable state of things? Is it either followed or preceded by a desirable state of things?

When any of those accidents occur by which the annual produce is for one year, or a few years, reduced considerably below the usual standard, in a country in which a considerable proportion of the people have better incomes than those who live upon wages, considerable savings may be made from their expenditure, to mitigate the effects of the deficiency. In a country in which all were reduced to the state of wages, any considerable diminution of the usual supply would diffuse general, irremediable calamity.

All the blessings, which flow from that grand and distinguishing attribute of our nature, its progress-iveness, the power of advancing continually from one degree of knowledge, one degree of command over the means of happiness, to another, seem, in a great measure, to depend upon the existence of a class of men who have their time at their command; that is, who are rich enough to be freed from all solicitude with respect to the means of living in a certain state of en-joyment. It is by this class of men that knowledge is cultivated and enlarged; it is also by this class that it is diffused; it is this class of men whose chil-dren receive the best education, and are prepared for all the higher and more delicate functions of society, as legislators, judges, administrators, teachers, inven-tors in all the arts, and superintendents in all the more important works, by which the dominion of the human species is extended over the powers of nature.

It is also, in a peculiar manner, the business of those whose object it is to ascertain the means of raising human happiness to its greatest height, to consider, what is that class of men by whom the greatest hap-piness is enjoyed. It will not probably be disputed, that they who are raised above solicitude for the means of subsistence and respectability, without being exposed to the vices and follies of great riches, the men of middling fortunes, in short, the men to whom society is generally indebted for its greatest improvements, are the men, who, having their time at their own disposal, freed from the necessity of manual labour, subject to no man's authority, and engaged in the most delightful occupations, obtain, as a class, the greatest sum of human enjoyment. For the happiness, therefore, as well as the ornament of our nature, it is peculiarly desirable that a class of this description should form as large a proportion of each community as possible. For this purpose it is absolutely necessary that population should not, by a forced accumulation of capital, be made to go on, till the return to capital from the land is very small. To enable a considerable portion of the community to enjoy the advantages of leisure, the return to capital must evidently be large. There is a certain density of population which is convenient, both for social intercourse, and for that combination of powers by which the produce of labour is increased. When these advantages, however, are attained, there seems little reason to wish that population should proceed any further. If it does proceed further, instead of increasing the net revenue derived from the land and labour of the country, or that portion of the annual produce which exceeds what is necessary for replacing the capital consumed, and maintaining the labourers, it lessens that important fund, on the largeness of which the happiness of society to a great degree depends.

If we may, thus, infer, that human happiness cannot be secured by taking forcible methods to make capital increase as fast as population ; and if, on the other hand, it is certain, that where births take place, more numerous than are required to uphold a population corresponding to the state of capital, human happiness is impaired, it is immediately seen, that the grand practical problem is, To find the means of limiting the number of births. It has also appeared, that, beyond a certain state of density in the population, such as to afford in perfection the benefits of social intercourse, and of combined labour, it is not desirable that population should increase. The precise problem, therefore, is, to find the means of limiting births to that number which is necessary to keep up the population, without increasing it. Were that accomplished, while the return to capital from the land was yet high, the reward of the labourer would be ample, and a large surplus would still remain. If the natural laws of distribution were allowed to operate freely, the greater part of this net produce would find its way, in moderate portions, into the hands of a numerous class of persons, exempt from the necessity of labour, and placed in the most favourable circumstances both for the enjoyment of

F

happiness, and for the highest intellectual and moral attainments.

We have yet to mention, that government, instead of lending, may itself employ the capital which it forcibly creates. It is evident, however, that whether government employs this capital, or lends it to be employed by others, all the effects, which we have traced as arising necessarily from its increase, will be the same. The best mode, perhaps, which could be invented for employing, by government itself, a portion of the annual produce, forcibly taken from the owners, to accelerate the growth of capital, would be that which has been so earnestly pressed upon the public attention by Mr. Owen, of New Lanark. Mr. Owen proposes, that the portion of the annual produce thus converted into capital should be employed by government in making certain establishments; each of a mixed nature, partly for agricultural, partly for manufacturing industry; in erecting the houses, in providing the instruments or machinery, the previous subsistence, and raw materials which might be required. In these establishments, Mr. Owen is of opinion that labour might be employed under great advantages, and with unexampled means of felicity to the individuals employed. Mr. Owen, however, must intend one of two things;—either that population should go on, or that it should stop. If it is to go on, capital of course holding pace with it, all the evils which would, as above, result from the forcible increase of capital, when lent by government, would result from its forcible increase, when employed in those establishments. If Mr. Owen means that population should not go on, and if expedients can be employed to limit sufficiently the number of births, there is no occasion for these establishments, still less for the forcible and painful abduction of a part of their income from the people. The limitation of the number of births, by raising wages, will accomplish every thing which we desire, without trouble and without interference. The limitation of the numbers, if that object can be attained, may be carried so far as not only to raise the condition of the labourer to any state of comfort and enjoyment which may be desired, but to prevent entirely the accumulation of capital.

SECTION III.

PROFITS.

WHEN it is established, that the whole of the annual produce is distributed as rent, wages of labour, and profits of stock; and when we have ascertained what regulates the portion which goes to rent, and what the portion which goes to wages, the question is also determined with regard to profits of stock; for it is evident that the portion which remains is profits.

From preceding expositions, it appears, that rent is something altogether extraneous to what may be considered as the return to the productive operations of capital and labour. As soon as it is necessary to apply capital to land of an inferior quality, or upon the same land to apply a further dose of capital with inferior return, all that is yielded, more than this inferior return, is as if it did not exist, with respect to the capitalist and labourer. Whatever is yielded beyond this lowest return, either on particular spots of ground, or to particular portions of capital, might be annihilated, the moment it is produced, without affecting the portion which goes to either of those two classes. As soon as a new portion of capital is employed with inferior return, the case would be the same, if the productive powers of all the capital employed upon the land were reduced to this inferior return, and a quantity of produce, equal to the additional return, which used to be made, to the former portions of capital, were, by miracle, rained down from heaven upon the possessors of the land which yielded it.

The portion, which goes, in the shape of rent, to the landlord, and which is an excess beyond the return made to the whole of the capital and labour employed upon the land, is, in fact, the result of an accident. Suppose that all the land cultivated in the country were of one uniform quality, and yielded the same return to every portion of the capital employed upon it, with the exception of one acre. That acre, we shall suppose, yields six times as much as any other acre. What would be produced upon all the other acres, might justly be regarded as the return made to the labour and capital employed upon the land; and the whole of that return. The additional five-sixths, accruing from the singular acre, would not be considered as return made to labour and capital; it would be considered as the accidental product of a particular virtue in that particular spot. But what is true of this single acre is equally true of any number of acres, as soon as that event occurs which diminishes the return to any portion of capital, and induces all the owners of capital to limit their profits to the measure of that diminished return.

If there is any portion of capital, employed upon the land, which pays no rent, it is evident that the wages and profits, in that case, must regulate the wages and profits in other cases.

It thus fully appears, that nothing can be considered as the produce of the joint operations of capital and labour upon the land, beyond the return to that portion of capital which is applied without paying any rent, which return measures the quantity of the produce allowed to remain, after the rent is deducted, as the return to all the other portions of labour and capital employed upon the land. The whole of that therefore, which can be considered as the real product of labour and capital, remains to be shared between the labourer and capitalist, after the rent is withdrawn. It follows that, in considering what regulates wages and profits, rent may be left altogether out of the question. Rent is the effect, and not the cause, of the diminished produce which the capitalists and labourers have to divide between them.

When any thing is to be divided wholly between two parties, that which regulates the share of one, regulates also, it is very evident, the share of the other; for whatever is withheld from the one, the other receives; whatever, therefore, increases the share of the one diminishes that of the other, and *vice versâ.* We might, therefore, with equal propriety, it should seem, affirm that wages determine profits, or that profits determine wages; and, in framing our language, assume whichever we pleased, as the regulator or standard.

As we have seen, however, that the regulation of the shares between the capitalist and labourer depends upon the relative abundance of population and capital, and that population, as compared with capital, has a tendency to superabound, the active principle of change is on the side of population, and constitutes a reason for considering population, and consequently wages, as the regulator.

As, therefore, the profits of stock depend upon the share, which is received by its owners, of the joint produce of labour and stock; profits of stock depend upon wages; rise as wages fall, and fall as wages rise.

In speaking of the produce which is shared between the capitalist and labourer, it is proper to explain, that I always mean such net produce as remains after replacing the capital which has been consumed. As, in stating the constituents of price, we say that a commodity must fetch in the market a value equal to three things: 1st, to the capital which has been consumed in its production; 2dly, to the ordinary profits of stock upon the capital employed; and, 3dly, to the wages of the labour; so in speaking of the portions into which, as the produce to be shared, the commodity or commodity's worth is to be considered as dividing itself, we must set apart the portion, always a determinate amount, which is for the capital consumed, and which is distinct both from profits and from wages. Thus, if in the production of a commodity, which sells for 100*l*., capital to the amount of 50*l*. has been consumed, 50*l*. is that which is to be divided between the capitalist and labourer, as profits to the one, and wages to the other.

The terms alteration of wages, alteration of profits, are susceptible of various meanings, to which it is necessary to advert.

1. If, by alteration, is meant, a change in the proportions, it is evident that an alteration of one share implies an alteration of the other; and the proposition that profits depend upon wages, admits of no qualification.

2. If a change in the quantity of commodities is meant, it will not be true, in that sense, that profits so depend upon wages, as to fall when wages rise, and rise when wages fall; for both may fall, and both may rise, together. And this is a proposition which no political economist has called in question. If the powers of production are either increased or diminished, there will, in the one case, be more, in the other less, to divide. The proportions remaining the same, both wages and profits will, in the one case, be raised, in the other, depressed.

The terms may have another meaning still. When a change in wages and profits is spoken of, it may be the value of what is received under these denominations, which is meant to be indicated.

To perceive what may, and what may not, be truly predicated or spoken of the terms in this sense, it is necessary to advert to a double meaning of the word value.

1. It is used in the sense of value in exchange; as when we say, that the value of a hat is double that of a handkerchief, if one hat will exchange for two handkerchiefs.

2. Mr. Ricardo, in his exposition of the principles of political economy, used the word value in a sense referable, not to purchasing power, but to cost of production. Thus, if two days' labour went to the production of one commodity, and two to the production of another commodity, Mr. Ricardo would say, the two commodities were of equal value. In like manner, if two days' labour produced at one time a certain amount of commodities, and at another time, by an improvement in the productive powers of that labour, a greater amount of commodities, Mr. Ricardo would say that the value of the smaller quantity, and the value of the greater quantity, were the same.

If we use the term value in the sense of exchangeable value, or purchasing power; that is, command over a greater or less quantity of commodities; the case is the same with that which we have already considered, wherein rise and fall of wages or profits were taken to mean, a greater or less amount of commodities. When we say that the labourer receives a greater quantity of commodities, and when we say that he receives a greater exchangeable value, we denote by the two expressions, one and the same thing. In this sense, therefore, nobody has ever maintained that profits necessarily rise when wages fall, and fall when wages rise: because it was always easy to see, that, by an alteration in productive power, both may rise or fall together, and also that one may rise or fall, and the other remain stationary.

We come next to consider what language may be correctly used, in the sense which Mr. Ricardo annexed to the word value.

It will immediately be seen that, in this sense, the case corresponds exactly with the first of those which I have already considered, that of proportions. If what is produced, by an invariable quantity of labour, continues to be divided in the same proportion, say one half to the capitalist, and one half to the labourers, that half may be a greater or a smaller quantity of commodities, but it will always be the produce of the same quantity of labour; and, in Mr. Ricardo's sense, always, for that reason, of the same value. In this sense of the word value, therefore, it is strictly and undeniably true, that profits depend upon wages so as to rise when wages fall, and fall when wages rise.

In the common mode of expressing profits, the reference that is made is not to the produced commodity, but to the capital employed in producing it; including the wages, which it is necessary to advance, and from which the owner expects of course to derive the same advantage as from his other advances. Profits are expressed not in aliquot parts of the produce, but of this capital. It is not so much per cent of the produce that a capitalist is said to receive, but so much per cent upon his capital. Now, the capital may be either of more, or of less value than the produce, according to the proportion in which it is capital of the fixed, or the circulating kind. Suppose a capital of 200l. of which 50l. is consumed in the production of a commodity, which sells for 120l.; we have first to deduct 50l. for the capital consumed; there then remains 70l. to be divided between the capitalist and the labourers; and if we suppose that 50l. has been paid for wages, in other words, that such is the share of the labourers, the capitalist receives 10 per cent upon his capital; including here, in the term capital, what he has advanced as wages; but he receives $28\frac{1}{2}$ per cent of the produce, or of that which is divided after replacing the capital consumed. It is only, however, the language which here is different; the thing expressed is precisely the same; and whether the capitalist says he receives 10 per cent upon his capital, or 28½ per cent of the produce, he means in both cases the same amount, viz. 20*l.*

There are, therefore, in reality, but two cases. The one, that in which we speak of proportions; the other, that in which we speak of quantity of commodities. In the one case, it is correct to say that profits depend literally and strictly upon wages. In the other case, although it is still correct to say that profits depend upon wages; for the greater the share that goes to the labourer, the less the share that remains for the capitalist; yet to make the language of quantity correspond in meaning with the language of proportions, the form of expression requires to be modified.

There is a great convenience in adapting our language to the rate upon the capital, rather than the shares of the produce; because the rate upon the capital is the same in all the varieties of produce, but the share of the capitalist is different, according to all the different degrees in which capital contributes to the intended result.

This, however, it is evident, makes no difference in the truth of the doctrine. If in one case capital contributes twice as much, in another three times as much, as it does in a third case, whatever share the capitalist in the third case receives, the capitalist in the first case will receive twice as great a share, and the capitalist in the second case will receive three times as great ; if the share of the capitalist in the third case is reduced one third by rise of wages, the share of each of the other two will also be reduced one third ; and whatever, in percentage on his capital, the profits of the one are reduced, the same in that percentage will the profits of the others be reduced.

As this percentage however is generally spoken in the sense of exchangeable value, it may happen, as we have seen above, that the shares may be altered without an alteration of this percentage. If, at the same time that the shares of the capitalists are reduced, by a rise of wages, there should happen an increase of the productive powers of labour and capital, the reduced shares might consist of as great a quantity of commodities as the previous shares, and of course the exchangeable value, and percentage on the capital, expressed in the language of exchangeable value, would remain the same.

If it should be deemed a better mode of expounding the subject, not to regard, as a separate portion, what is required to replace the capital consumed, but to consider it as forming part of the share of the capitalist; the same propositions will still be true. The whole which is to be divided will, in this case, be different from the former whole, and the shares will not be the same proportion of that whole ; but it will still be true that by how much the proportion of the labourers is increased, by so much that of the capitalist will be reduced; and that when the capitalist has set apart that portion of his share which is required to replace his capital, his profits, or the advantage upon the use of his capital, will be affected, precisely as they are said to be according to the former mode of exposition.

If we speak of what accrues to the two parties in the language of quantity, not of proportion, it is equally clear, in this mode of exposition as in the former, that the quantity of commodities is not necessarily altered when the shares are altered ; that the shares may alter when there is no alteration in the quantity of produce to be shared ; and, on the other hand, that the quantity of produce to be shared may alter, either up or down, while the shares are the same. It is, at the same time, true, that there can be no alteration in the quantity of produce which the one receives, but by an alteration in the quantity which the other receives ; unless in that one case, in which the productive powers of the instruments of production have undergone alteration. The following, therefore, is a connected chain of true propositions.

1. That which accrues to the parties concerned in

the production of a commodity or commodities, the labourers, and capitalist, as the return for their co-operation, is a share of the produce to each.

2. The share of the one cannot be increased, without a corresponding diminution of the share of the other.

3. These shares remaining the same, the quantity of produce included in them may be either greater or less, according as the productive operations have been followed with a greater or a smaller produce.

4. According as you apply the term value, to the effect, the quantity of produce ; or to the cause, the quantity of labour employed; it will be true, or it will not be true, that the value of what is received by the capitalist the labourer and reciprocates along with their shares.

It is equally easy, in this mode of expression as in the former, to translate the language of shares into that of percentage. The amount of the produce, or its exchangeable value, may be greater, or may be less, than the amount of capital employed. If the capital is all circulating capital, and consumed in the process of production, and if, as in ordinary language, we suppose wages to be included, the produce is greater than the capital, by the amount of the profits. Let us suppose that the capital is 500*l*.,

and profits 10 per cent; the value of the produce is
550*l.*; let us suppose that of this the capitalist
pays 275*l.* in wages; in other words, that the labourers' share is 50 per cent; it follows, that the share
of the capitalist is 50 per cent also; but 50 per cent
of 550*l.* is a greater amount than 50 per cent of
his capital, which is only 500*l.* This is equal to 55
per cent upon his capital. And when he has deducted from his share, what is necessary to replace
the portion of his capital, otherwise consumed than
in the payment of wages, viz. 500*l.* — 275*l.* = 225*l.*,
he has 50*l.* remaining, or 10 per cent upon his
capital.

Let us next take the case in which the capital
500*l.*, as before, is all fixed capital, none of it, excepting
what is advanced as wages, consumed; that this is
small, viz. 25*l.*; and that the value of the commodity
is 75*l.*; of this, 25*l.*, or $\frac{1}{3}$, is the share of the labourer;
50*l.*, or $\frac{2}{3}$, is the share of the capitalist; but this, though
$66\frac{1}{2}$ per cent upon the product, is but '10 per cent
upon the capital.

There is a mode of viewing the gross return to the
capitalist, which has a tendency to simplify our
language, and, so far, has a great advantage to re-
commend it. The case of fixed and of circulating
capital may be treated as the same, by merely considering the fixed capital as a product, which is regularly consumed and replaced, by every course of

productive operations. The capital, not consumed, may be always taken, as an additional commodity, the result of the productive process.

According to this supposition, the share of the capitalist is always equal to the whole of his capital, together with its profits.

We may consider capital in two senses; first, as including; next, as excluding, wages.

In the first case, let us suppose a capital, of 500*l.*, of which 100*l.* is paid in wages, to produce a commodity worth 550*l.* The share of the capitalist is 450*l.* or somewhat more than four-fifths, while that of the labourers is so much less than one-fifth; and the profit of stock, after replacing capital, is 10 per cent.

Let us suppose, in the second case, a capital of 400*l.*, but exclusive of wages. This capital is employed, and the necessary labourers maintain themselves without wages, and take, as their remuneration, their share of the commodity when produced. The commodity is worth 550*l.*; and of that 100*l.* falls to the share of the labourers. The rate of profits is the same as before, and the proportions are the same as before, only with this correction, that in the former case the labourers sustained a discount of 10 per cent.

upon their share, on account of anticipated payment. The real shares in both cases are four-fifths to the capitalist, and one-fifth to the workmen.

It is sufficiently evident that, so long as the capital and the labour remain the same, and the shares remain the same, so long, in Mr. Ricardo's sense of the word value, will the same value accrue to each, whether the quantity of produce they receive be greater or less.

That the capital, and the labour, should remain the same, is as necessary a condition, as that the shares should remain the same; for if either is increased or diminished, the value of the product, in Mr. Ricardo's sense of the word value, is also increased or diminished.

The quantity of produce being supposed the same, we may illustrate the subject by the following cases.

1. Let us suppose that both capital and labour are diminished, and in equal proportions. This is precisely the same with the case in which the productive powers of labour and capital are increased; as it comes to the same thing, whether you have the same produce from a less cost of production, or a greater produce from the same cost of production. This case, therefore, has been already considered.

2. Let us suppose, that the capital is diminished, the labour not. This also is a case of diminished cost of production. If, for the produce of 550 yards of cloth, which was at first effected by a capital of 400 yards and a portion of labour which was paid by a fifth of the produce, only a capital of 200 yards should be required, but the same quantity of immediate labour; that the labourers may have the same share as before, it is necessary that they should have a greater aliquot part. Suppose, before that increase of productive power which is supposed in this case, when a capital of 400 yards was required for a produce of 550, and when the wages of the quantity of labour applied was 110 yards, that another commodity had been produced by the same quantity of labour, but by a capital of 200 yards. The value of this commodity would have been 330 yards, equal to the capital with its profits and the wages. Of this the labourers would have received 110 yards, or one-third. This is the same proportion to a capital of 200 yards, as one-fifth is to a capital of 400 yards. If the labour contributed one-fifth to the product of 550 yards, when aided by a capital of 400 yards, it contributes one-third, in the newly supposed case, when aided by a capital of 200 yards. One-third of 550 is $183\frac{1}{3}$; leaving to the capitalist $366\frac{2}{3}$, or a profit upon his capital of $83\frac{1}{3}$ per cent. According to the explanation, which we have already given and repeated, there is here an additional produce to each, by reason of the increase of productive

·power; and, also, which is only the same thing in other words, an augmented value in exchange. But in Mr. Ricardo's sense of the word value, there is only the same value to each, so long as the proportions remain unchanged.

The cases which I have thus put for illustration, are cases in which the productive powers of labour and capital are augmented; but as the same reasonings apply, *mutatis mutandis*, to the cases in which the productive powers are diminished, it is deemed unnecessary to lengthen this analysis by adducing them.

It may here be useful to the learner to look back, and ascertain the number and importance of the steps which he has advanced. He has discovered, what are the laws, according to which those commodities, which form the riches of nations, are produced; and what are the laws, according to which, when produced, they are distributed.

He has seen that there are two instruments of production; one primary, the other secondary: that labour is the primary instrument of production, and that, abstracted from those aids which it derives from capital, its productive powers are augmented chiefly by limiting the number of each man's productive operations; in other words, by what has been called the division of labour: that capital is secondary to labour, not only because it is subsequent in order of time, but because it owes its existence to labour; because the first capital is the result of pure labour, and because that which is subsequently the result of labour and capital combined, may thence be resolved into labour, the ultimate principle of all production.

The learner has now also seen, that, what is produced, by the operations of labour and capital, divides itself, in the first instance, into three portions; the rent of land; the wages of labour; and the profits of stock. Till the laws were discovered, which determine the boundaries of these several portions, that which goes as rent, that which goes as profits, and that which goes as wages, almost all the conclusions of Political Economy were vague and uncertain. It has been seen, that rent is something which may be considered independent of the general result of the productive powers of labour and capital; that it is the result of a peculiar defect of the earth, which does not continue to yield its produce in equal abundance to successive portions of capital; and that it is the excess of what is yielded to the more productive portions, above what is equal to the produce of the least productive portion of capital employed upon the land. After the limits were thus fixed of this one of the three portions, into which the produce of industry divides itself, whence it appeared that what may be regarded as the genuine effect of labour and capital in co-operation is left to be divided between the labourer and the capitalist; it was easy for the learner to see, that, in respect to proportions, as what fell to the share of the one was increased, what went to the share of the other was diminished, and that in this sense, wages and profits depend on one another; that in respect, however, to the quantity of produce which these shares may contain, the productive power of the instruments of production is the determining cause.

CHAPTER III.

INTERCHANGE.

SECTION I.

NATURE OF THE ADVANTAGE DERIVED FROM THE INTERCHANGE OF COMMODITIES, AND THE PRINCIPAL AGENTS EMPLOYED IN IT.

WHEN two men have more than they need; one, for example, of food; another, of cloth; while the first desires more of cloth than he possesses, the second more of food; it is a great accommodation to both, if they can perform an exchange of a part of the food of the one for a part of the cloth of the other; and so in other cases.

In performing exchanges, there are two sets of persons, the intervention of whom is of great advantage : the first are Carriers, the second Merchants.

When the division and distribution of labour has been carried to any considerable extent, goods are produced at some, often at a very considerable, distance from the place where they are wanted for consumption. It is necessary that they should be conveyed from the one place to the other. Carriers are of two sorts : Carriers by Land, and Carriers by Water. For the business of carriage, both capital and labour are required. In carriage by land, the waggons or carts, the horses or other cattle, and the maintenance both of them and of the necessary number of men ; in carriage by water, the ships, and the maintenance of the men who navigate them, constitute the capital required.

To procure articles, as men have occasion to consume them, it would be very inconvenient to repair, in each instance, to the respective manufacturers and producers, who may often live at a very considerable distance from one another. Great trouble is saved to consumers, when they find assembled in one place the whole, or any considerable portion, of the articles which they use. This convenience gives rise to the class of merchants, who buy from the manufacturers, and keep ready for use, all those articles for which they expect a profitable sale.

In small towns, where one or a few merchants can supply the wants of all the population, the shop or store of one merchant contains articles of all, or most of the kinds, in general demand. In places where the population is large, instead of a great number of shops, each dealing in almost all kinds of articles, it is found more convenient to divide the articles into classes, and that each shop should confine itself to a particular class : one, for example, to hats, another to hosiery; one to glass, another to iron; and so on.

SECTION II.

WHAT DETERMINES THE QUANTITY IN WHICH COMMODITIES EXCHANGE FOR ONE ANOTHER.

WHEN a certain quantity of one commodity is exchanged for a certain quantity of another commodity; a certain quantity of cloth, for example, for a certain quantity of corn; there is something which determines the owner of the cloth to accept for it such and such a quantity of corn; and, in like manner, the owner of the corn to accept such and such a quantity of cloth.

This is, evidently, the principle of demand and supply, in the first instance. If a great quantity of corn comes to market to be exchanged for cloth, and only a small quantity of cloth to be exchanged for corn, a great quantity of corn will be given for a small quantity of cloth. If the quantity of cloth, which thus comes to market, is increased, without any increase in the quantity of corn, the quantity of corn which is exchanged for a given quantity of cloth will be proportionally diminished.

This answer, however, does not resolve the whole of the question. The quantity in which commodities exchange for one another depends upon the proportion of supply to demand. It is evidently therefore necessary to ascertain upon what that proportion depends. What are the laws according to which supply is furnished to demand, is one of the most important inquiries in Political Economy.

Demand creates, and the loss of demand annihilates, supply. When an increased demand arises for any commodity, an increase of supply, if the supply is capable of increase, follows, as a regular effect. If the demand for any commodity altogether ceases, the commodity is no longer produced.

The connexion here, of causes and effects, is easily explained. If corn is brought to market, the cost of bringing it has been so much. If cloth is brought to market, the cost of bringing it has been so much. For the benefit of simplicity, the number of commodities in the market is here supposed to be two: it is of no consequence, with regard to the result, whether they are understood to be few or many.

The cost of bringing the corn to market has been either equal to that of bringing the cloth, or unequal. If it has been equal, there is no motive, to those who bring the cloth or the corn, for altering the quantity of either. They cannot obtain more of the commodity which they receive in exchange, by transferring their labour to its production. If the cost has been unequal, there immediately arises a motive for altering the proportions. Suppose that the cost of bringing the whole of the corn has been greater than that of bringing the whole of the cloth; and that the whole of the one is exchanged against the whole of the other, either at once, or in parts: the persons who brought the cloth have in that case possessed themselves of a quantity of corn at less cost, than that at which it was brought to market, by those who produced it; those, on the other hand, who brought the corn have possessed themselves of a quantity of cloth, at a greater cost than that at which it can be made and brought to market.

Here motives arise, to diminish the quantity of corn, and increase the quantity of cloth; because the men who have been producing corn, and purchasing cloth, can obtain more cloth, by transferring their means of production from the one to the other. As soon, again, as no more cloth can be obtained by applying the same amount of means to the production of cloth, than by applying them to corn, and exchanging it for cloth, all motive to alter the quantity of the one as compared with that of the other is at an end. Nothing is to be gained by producing corn rather than cloth, or cloth rather than corn. The cost of production on both sides is equal.

It thus appears that the relative value of commodities, or in other words, the quantity of one which exchanges for a given quantity of another, depends upon demand and supply, in the first instance; but upon cost of production, ultimately; and hence, in accurate language, upon cost of production, entirely. An increase or diminution of demand or supply, may temporarily increase or diminish, beyond the point of productive cost, the quantity of one commodity which exchanges for a given quantity of another; but the law of competition, wherever it is not obstructed, tends invariably to bring it to that point, and to keep it there.

Cost of production, then, regulates the exchangeable value of commodities. But cost of production is itself involved in some obscurity.

Two instruments are commonly combined in production; Labour and Capital.

It follows, either that cost of production consists in labour and capital combined; or that one of these may be resolved into the other. If one of them can be resolved into the other, it follows that cost of production does not consist in both combined.

The opinion, which is suggested by first appearances, undoubtedly is, that cost of production consists in capital alone. The capitalist pays the wages of his labourer, buys the raw material, and expects that what he has expended shall be returned to him, in the price, with the ordinary profits upon the whole of the capital employed. From this view of the subject, it would appear, that cost of production consists exclusively in the portion of capital expended, together with the profits upon the whole of the capital employed in effecting the production.

It is easy, however, to see, that in the term capital, thus understood, an ambiguity, and hence a fallacy, is involved. When we say that capital and labour, the two instruments of production, belong to two classes of persons; we mean that the labourers have contributed so much to the production, and the capitalists so much; and that the commodity, when produced, belongs in certain proportions to both. It may so happen, however, that one of these parties has purchased the share of the other, before the production is completed. In that case, the whole of the commodity belongs to the party who has purchased the share of the other. In point of fact, it does happen, that the capitalist, as often as he employs labourers, by the payment of wages, purchases the share of the labourers. When the labourers receive wages for their labour, without waiting to be paid by a share of the commodity produced, it is evident that they sell their title to that share. The capitalist is then the owner, not of the capital only, but of the labour also. If what is paid as wages is included, as it commonly is, in the term capital, it is absurd to talk of labour separately from capital.   The word capital, as thus employed, includes labour and capital both. To say, therefore, that the exchangeable value of commodities is determined by capital, understood in this sense, is to say that it is determined by labour and capital combined.   This, however, is returning to the point from which we set out. It is nugatory to include labour in the definition of the word capital, and then to say that, capital without labour, determines exchangeable value.   If capital is understood in a sense which does not include the purchase money of labour, and hence the labour itself, it is obvious that capital does not regulate the exchangeable value of commodities.

If labour were the sole instrument of production, and capital not required, the produce of one day's labour in one commodity would exchange against the produce of one day's labour in another commodity. In the rude state of society, if the hunter and the fisherman desired to vary their food, the one by a portion of game, the other by a portion of fish, the average quantity which they took in a day would form the standard of exchange. If it did not, one of the two would be placed in a more unfavourable situation than his neighbour, with perfect power, which he would of course employ, to pass from the one situation to the other.

In estimating equal quantities of labour, an allowance would, of course, be included for different degrees of hardness and skill.   If the products of each of two days' labour of equal hardness and skill exchanged for one another, the product of a day's labour, which was either harder, or required a greater degree of skill, would exchange for something more.

All capital consists really in commodities.   The capital of the farmer is not the money which he may be worth, because that he cannot apply to production.   His capital consists in his implements and stock.

As all capital consists in commodities, it follows, of course, that the first capital must have been the result of pure labour.   The first commodities could not be made by any commodities existing before them.

But if the first commodities, and of course the first capital, were the result of pure labour, the value of this capital, the quantity of other commodities for which it would exchange, must have been estimated by labour.   This is an immediate consequence of the proposition which we have just established, that where labour was the sole instrument of production, exchangeable value was determined by the quantity of labour which the production of the commodity required.

If this be established, it is a necessary consequence, that the exchangeable value of all commodities is determined by quantity of labour.

The first capital, as has just been seen, being the result of pure labour, bears a value in proportion to that labour. This capital concurs in production. And it is contended that as soon as capital concurs in production, the value of the commodity produced is determined by the value of the capital. But the value of that capital itself, we have just observed, is determined by labour. To say, therefore, that the value of a product is determined by the value of the capital, is of no use, when you have to go beyond the value of the capital, and ask, what it is by which that value is itself determined. To say that the value of the product is determined by the value of the capital, but the value of the capital is determined by the quantity of labour, is to say that the value of the product is determined by the quantity of labour.

It thus undeniably appears, that not only the value of the first capital, but, by equal necessity, that of the commodities which are produced by the first capital, is determined by quantity of labour. Capital of the second stage must consist in the commodities which are produced by that of the first stage. It must, therefore, be estimated by the quantity of labour. The same reasoning applies to it in every

H

subsequent stage. The value of the first capital was regulated by quantity of labour : the value of that which was produced by the first capital was regulated by the value of the first : that, however, was valued by labour : the last, therefore, is valued by labour ; and so on, without end, as often as successive productions may be supposed to be made. But, if the value of all capital must be determined by labour, it follows, upon all suppositions, that the value of all commodities must be determined by labour.

To say, indeed, that the value of commodities depends upon capital, implies one of the most obvious of all absurdities. Capital is commodities. If the value of commodities, then, depends upon the value of capital, it depends upon the value of commodities ; value in short depends upon value. This is not an exposition of value. It is an attempt clearly and completely abortive.

It thus appears, that quantity of labour, in the last resort, determines the proportion in which commodities exchange for one another.

There is one phenomenon which is brought to controvert these conclusions, and which it is, therefore, necessary to explain.

It is said that the exchangeable value of commodities is affected by time, without the intervention of labour; because, when profits of stock must be included, so much must be added for every portion of time which the production of one commodity requires beyond that of another. For example, if the same quantity of labour has produced in the same season a cask of wine, and 20 sacks of flour, they will exchange against one another at the end of the season: but if the owner of the wine places the wine in his cellar, and keeps it for a couple of years, it will be worth more than the 20 sacks of flour, because the profits of stock for the two years must be added to the original price. Here is an addition of value, but here it is affirmed, there has been no new application of labour; quantity of labour, therefore, is not the principle by which exchangeable value is regulated.

This objection is founded upon a misapprehension with respect to the nature of profits. Profits are, in reality, the measure of quantity of labour; and the only measure of quantity of labour to which, in the case of capital, we can resort. This can be established by rigid analysis.

If two commodities are produced, a bale of silk, for example, for immediate consumption, and a machine, which is an article of fixed capital; it is certain, that if the bale of silk and the machine were produced by the same quantity of labour, and in the same time, they would exactly exchange for one

another : quantity of labour would clearly be the regulator of their value.

But suppose that the owner of the machine, instead of selling it, is disposed to use it, for the sake
of the profits which it brings ; what is the real character and nature of his action ? Instead of receiving
the price of his machine all at once, he takes a defer-
red payment, so much per annum : he receives, in
fact, an annuity, in lieu of the capital sum ; an annuity, fixed by the competition of the market, and
which is therefore an exact equivalent for the capital
sum.   Whatever the proportion which the capital
sum bears to the annuity, whether it be ten years'
purchase, or twenty years' purchase, such a proportion is each year's annuity of the original value of
the machine.   The conclusion, therefore, is incontro-
vertible : as the exchangeable value of the machine,
had it been sold as soon as made, would have been
the practical measure of the quantity of labour employed in making it, one-tenth or one-twentieth of
that value measures also a tenth or a twentieth of
the quantity of labour.

If a piece of machinery, which has cost 100 days'
labour, is applied in making a commodity, and is
worn out in the making of it ; and if 100 days' pure
labour are employed in making another commodity ;
the produce of the machine, and the produce of the

labour, supposing no adjustment necessary for difference of time, will exchange against one another.

Make now a different supposition: that the machine is an article of fixed capital, and not worn out, and let us trace the consequences. It was correctly supposed, in the former case, that 100 days' labour were expended by wearing out the machine; but 100 days' labour have not been expended in the second, because the machine is not worn out. Some labour, however, has been expended, because 100 days' labour in a mass has been applied. How much of it shall we say has been expended? We have an exact measure of it in the equivalent which is paid. If the equivalent which was obtained when the machine was worn out, was a measure of 100 days' labour, whatever proportion of such equivalent is received as a year's use of the machine when not worn out, must represent a corresponding proportion of the labour expended upon the machine.

Capital is allowed to be correctly described under the title of hoarded labour. A portion of capital produced by 100 days' labour, is 100 days' hoarded labour. But the whole of the 100 days' hoarded labour is not expended, when the article constituting the capital is not worn out. A part is expended, and what part? Of this we have no direct, we have only an indirect measure. If capital, paid for by an annuity, is paid for at the rate of 10 per cent, one-tenth of the hoarded labour may be correctly considered as expended in one year.

The instance which is commonly adduced as exemplifying the supposed fact of an increase of value without increase of labour, is that of wine. Wine acquires a greater value by being merely deposited in the cellars of the merchant.

But they who would advance this, as an answer to the antecedent reasoning, do not perceive the force of their own objection. Their doctrine is, that exchangeable value is regulated by cost of production. Cost of production is the outlay necessary for completing the product. When the wine was put into the cellar, it was worth so much, according to the capital expended in its production. When it is placed in the cellar, no more capital is employed upon it, nor any more labour; and yet it acquires an additional value. The question, why it acquires more value, when there is not more capital, is just as difficult, as why it acquires more value, when there is not more labour.

It is no solution to say, that profits must be paid; because this only brings us to the question, why must profits be paid? To this there is no answer but one, that they are the remuneration for labour; labour not applied immediately to the commodity in question, but applied to it through the medium of other commodities, the produce of labour. Thus a man has a machine, the produce of 100 days' labour. In applying it, the owner undoubtedly applies labour, though in a secondary sense, by applying that which could not have been had but through the medium of labour. This machine, let us suppose, is calculated to last exactly 10 years. One tenth of the fruits of 100 days' labour is thus expended every year; which is the same thing in the view of cost and value, as saying that 10 days' labour have been expended. The owner is to be paid for the 100 days' labour which the machine costs him, at the rate of so much per annum, that is, by an annuity for ten years, equivalent to the original value of the machine. It thus appears that profits are simply remuneration for labour. They may, indeed, without doing any violence to language, hardly even by a metaphor, be denominated wages : the wages of that labour which is applied, not immediately by the hand, but mediately, by the instruments which the hand has produced. And if you may measure the amount of immediate labour by the amount of wages, you may measure the amount of secondary labour by that of the return to the capitalist. We surely have not occasion to add, that if this be the general account of profits, which seems undeniable, it is applicable to all particular cases, to that of wine in the cellar, as well as to every other. Suppose that 100 men make a machine in one day, that another 100 men employ this machine the next day, and wear it out;

the first 100 men, and the second 100 men, will divide the produce equally between them. The share of the first 100 men is payment for capital, no doubt, but it is also, most obviously, payment for labour too; and in whatever degree labour is productive, that is, yields more than is consumed in effecting the product, to that degree an advantage is afforded beyond the replacing of the capital consumed, and constitutes profit.

The return which is made to capital employed upon the land, is that which determines the rate of annual profit from all other employments of capital; and, of course, for that which is employed in meliorating wine in a wine-cellar. The case of the wine in the cellar coincides exactly with that of a machine worn out in a year, which works by itself without additional labour. The new wine, which is one machine, is replaced by its produce, the old wine, with that addition of value which corresponds with the return to capital employed upon the land; and the account which is to be rendered of the one return, is also the true account of the other.

SECTION III.

EFFECT UPON EXCHANGEABLE VALUES OF A FLUCTUATION IN WAGES AND PROFITS.

IN stating that commodities are produced by two instruments, Labour and Capital, of which the last is the result of labour, we, in effect, mean, that commodities are produced by two quantities of labour, differently circumstanced; the one, immediate, or primary labour, that which is applied at once by the hand of the labourer; the other, hoarded, or secondary labour, that which is the result of former labour, and either is applied in aid of the immediate labour, or is the subject matter upon which it is bestowed.

Of these two species of labour, two things are to be observed : First, that they are not always paid according to the same rate; that is, the payment of the one does not rise when that of the other rises, or fall when that of the other falls : And, secondly, that they do not always contribute to the production of all commodities in equal proportions.

If there were any two species of labour, the wages of which did not rise and fall in the same proportion, and which, contributing to the production of all commodities, did not contribute to them all in equal degrees, this circumstance, of their not contributing in equal degrees, would create a difference in exchangeable values, as often as any fluctuation took place in the rate of wages.

If all commodities were produced by a portion of skilled, and a portion of unskilled labour, but the ratio which these portions bore to one another were different in different commodities; and if, as often as the wages of skilled labour rose, the wages of unskilled labour rose twice as much; it is very obvious, that, upon a rise of wages, those commodities, to the production of which a greater proportion of unskilled labour was applied, would rise in value as compared with those to which a less proportion was applied. It is also obvious, that, though this difference in the ratios according to which the wages of the two kinds of labour had altered, and in the proportions in which they were applied to the production of different commodities, would, upon a rise or fall in wages, alter the relative value of the commodities, it would do so, without in the least degree affecting the truth of the proposition, that quantity of labour determined exchangeable values.

The case is precisely the same when we consider that it is the two species of labour, called primary and secondary, which are applied in different proportions.

Three cases will conveniently exemplify the different degrees in which labour and capital respectively contribute to production. These are the two extreme cases, and the medium. The first is that of commodities which are produced by immediate labour alone without capital ; the second, that of commodities produced, one half by capital, one half by immediate labour ; the third, that of commodities produced by capital alone without immediate labour. There are perhaps no actual cases which perfectly coincide with either of the extremes. There are, however, cases which approximate to both ; and when the most simple are illustrated as examples, allowance can easily and correctly be made for the differences of the rest.

If two species of labour are employed in the production of commodities ; and if, when the payment of the one species of labour rises, that of the other falls ; a commodity, in the production of which a greater proportion of the first species of labour is employed, will, upon a rise in the payment of that species of labour, rise in exchangeable value, as compared with a commodity in which less is employed. The degree however, in which it will rise, will depend upon two circumstances: first, upon the degree in which the payment of the one species of labour falls when the other rises ; and, secondly, upon the degree in which the proportion of the labour of the first kind, employed in its production, exceeds the proportion of it which is employed in the production of the other commodity.

The first question then, is, in what degree, when wages rise, do profits fall? And this is the only general question; for the degree in which the two species of labour combine in the production of different commodities, depends upon the circumstances of each particular case.

If all commodities corresponded with the first of the cases, assumed above as examples, and which we may, for the sake of abbreviation, designate, as No. 1, No. 2, No. 3; in other words, if all commodities were produced wholly by labour, capital being solely employed in the payment of wages; in that case, just as much as wages of labour rose, profits of stock would fall.

Suppose a capital of 1000*l.* to be thus employed, and profits to be 10 per cent., the value of the commodity would be 1100*l.*, for that would replace the capital with its profits. The commodity may be regarded as consisting of 1100 parts, of which 1000 would belong to the labourers, and 100 to the capitalist. Let wages, upon this, be supposed to rise 5 per cent.; in that case, it is evident, that instead of 100 parts of the 1100, the capitalist would receive only 50; his profits, therefore, instead of 10 would be only 5 per cent. Instead of 1000*l.* he would have to pay 1050*l.* in wages.   The commodity would not rise in value to indemnify him, because we have supposed that all commodities are in the same situation; it would, therefore, be of the value of 1100*l.*, as before, of which 50*l.* alone would remain for himself.

If all commodities corresponded with the case No. 2, profits would fall only half as much as wages rose.   If we suppose that 1000*l.* were paid in wages, and 1000*l.* employed in fixed capital; that profits, as before, were 10 per cent., and this the whole expenditure; the value of the commodity would be 1200*l.* because that is the sum which would replace the capital expended and pay the profits of the whole. In this case the commodity might be considered as divided into 1200 parts, of which 200 would belong to the capitalist.   If wages rose 5 per cent., and instead of 1000*l.* as wages, he paid 1050*l.* he would still retain 150*l.* as profits; in other words, he would sustain a reduction of only $2\frac{1}{2}$ per cent.

The case would be precisely the same, if we supposed the 1000*l.* of capital, which is not employed in the payment of wages, to be employed in any proportion, in the shape of circulating capital consumed in the course of the productive process, and requiring to be replaced.   Thus, while 1000*l.* were employed in the payment of wages, 500*l.* might be employed as fixed capital in durable machinery, 500*l.* in raw material and other expenses.   If this were the state of

the expenditure, the value of the article would be
1700*l.*; being the amount of the capital to be replaced, and 10 per cent. profits upon the whole. Of
these 1700 parts, 1000 would be the share of the labourers, though paid in advance, and 700 the share of
the capitalist, 200 being profits. If, now, wages were
to rise 5 per cent., 1050 of the above 1700 parts
would be the share of the labourers, and 650 only
would remain to the capitalist, of which, after replacing his 500*l.* of circulating capital, 150 would remain
as profits; a reduction of $2\frac{1}{2}$ per cent. as before.

If all commodities corresponded with the third
case, as no wages would be paid, profits could not be
affected by the rise of them : and it is obvious, that,
in proportion as commodities may be supposed to
approach that extreme, profits would be less and less
affected by such a rise.

If we suppose, what is most probable, that, in the
actual state of things, as many cases are on the one
side of the medium as on the other, the result would
be, in consequence of the mutual compensations that
would take place, that profits would be reduced
exactly half as much as wages rose.

The steps may be traced as follows :

When wages rise, and profits fall, it is evident
that all commodities, made with a less proportion of

labour to capital, will fall in value, as compared with those which are made with a greater.   Thus, if No. 1 is taken as the standard, that in which commodities are produced wholly by labour; all commodities belonging to that case will be said to remain of the same value; all belonging to any of the other cases will be said to fall in value.   If No. 2 is taken as the standard, all commodities appertaining to that case will be said to remain of the same value; all, belonging to any case nearer the first extreme, will be said to rise in value; all, to any nearer the last extreme, to fall.

Those capitalists, who produce articles of case No. 1, sustain, when wages have risen 5 per cent., an additional cost of 5 per cent.; but they exchange their commodity against other commodities.   If they exchange them against those of case No. 2, where the capitalists have sustained an additional cost of only $2\frac{1}{2}$ per cent., they will receive $2\frac{1}{2}$ per cent. additional quantity.   Thus, in obtaining goods, produced under the circumstances of case No. 2, they obtain a certain degree of compensation, and sustain, by the rise of wages, a disadvantage of noly $2\frac{1}{2}$ per cent.   In this exchange, however, the result, with respect to the capitalists who produce goods under the circumstances of case No. 2, is reversed.   They have already sustained a disadvantage of $2\frac{1}{2}$ per cent., in the production of their goods, and are made to sustain another disadvantage of $2\frac{1}{2}$ per cent. in obtaining, by exchange the goods produced uuder the circumstances of case No. 1.

The result, then, upon the whole, is, that all producers, who possess themselves, either by production or exchange, of goods produced under the circumstances of case No. 2, sustain a disadvantage of $2\frac{1}{2}$ per cent.; those who possess themselves of goods in cases approaching the first extreme, sustain a greater; those in cases approaching the last, a less disadvantage: that, if the cases on the one side are equal to those on the other, a loss of $2\frac{1}{2}$ per cent. is sustained upon the whole; that this, accordingly, is the extent to which, in practice, it may be supposed that profits are reduced.

From these elements it is easy to compute the effect of a rise of wages upon price. All commodities are compared with money, or the precious metals. If money be supposed to correspond with case No. 2, or to be produced, which is probably not far from the fact, by equal proportions of labour and capital; then all commodities, produced under these medium circumstances, are not altered in price by a rise of wages; those commodities which approach nearer the first extreme, or admit a greater proportion of labour than capital in their formation, rise in price: those which approach the second, that is, have a greater portion of capital than labour, fall: and, upon the aggregate of commodities or all taken together, there is neither fall nor rise.

From the explanations, here afforded, it will be easy to see what is meant by the term " measure of value," and wherein it differs from that which we have already endeavoured to explain, the " regulator of value."

Money, that is, the precious metals in coin, serves practically as a measure of value, as is evident from what has immediately been said. A certain quantity of the precious metal is taken as a known value, and the value of other things is measured by that value; one commodity is twice, another thrice the value of such a portion of the metal, and so on.

It is evident, however, that this can remain an accurate measure of value, only if it remains of the same value itself. If a commodity, which was twice the value of an ounce of silver, becomes three times its value, we can only know what change has taken place in the value of this commodity, if we know that our measure is unchanged.

But there is no commodity to be taken as a measure of value, which is not itself liable to alterations in value, or in its power of purchasing, from a change in the quantity of labour and capital required both for its own production, and that of other

I

commodities, and also from a change in wages and profits.

The alteration of value, arising from a change in the quantity of labour required for production, is the most important; for if we could be sure, that the commodity chosen for our measure of value was itself always produced under the same circumstances, that is, by the same quantity of immediate, and the same quantity of hoarded, labour, it would always answer the following purposes: 1st, it would show, by every alteration in its power of purchasing a commodity produced by the same proportion of labour and capital, the alteration which had taken place in the cost of production of that commodity, or in that by which its value is regulated: and 2dly, it might be accommodated by calculation to the changes in value, produced by the alteration of wages and profits, in the case of commodities not produced by the same proportions of labour and capital.

Thus, if gold were produced under the circumstances of case No. 1, by mere labour, picked up, for example, by the hand, from the beds of rivers, and always in equal quantity, in return for an equal quantity of labour, it would always be a measure, exactly and immediately, of all commodities produced by pure labour. In the case, however, of a rise of wages, and a fall in the profits of stock, gold would in these circumstances rise as compared with commodi.

ties produced under the circumstances of case No. 2, though no alteration should have taken place in the amount of the labour and capital required for their production. It is evident, therefore, that in these circumstances, gold, fluctuating in value with every fluctuation in the wages of labour, would very imperfectly serve the purposes of a measure of value. If a contract, for example, were made, to pay an annuity of so much gold for twenty years, it might be 10 per cent. more, or 10 per cent. less, at the end of that period, than it was at the beginning. Of labour it would all the time command exactly the same quantity, but of all commodities produced by aid of capital it would command a different quantity, and that, in proportion to the degree in which capital, not labour, was the instrument of their production.

Though we can by strict analysis discover, that exchangeable value is proportioned to quantity of labour expended in production, there are three circumstances which prevent its application as the measure of value.

In the first place, there are two kinds of labour employed in production, and the degree in which the produce is shared between them often varies, and occasions, as we have seen, a corresponding variation in the exchangeable values of commodities produced by different proportions of these two kinds of labour. In the next place, we have no practical means of ascertaining before hand the exact quantity of hoarded labour which goes to production, since the only measure we have of its quantity is the price which it brings. In the third place, labour is not constant in its productive powers. If one day's labour produced always the same quantity of gold, but not the same quantity of corn, or of cloth, the exchangeable value of gold would alter in respect to corn and cloth.

From these explanations it also appears, that nothing else can be applied as an accurate measure of value.

Every commodity may be considered as produced under one of the three sets of circumstances specified above. If we take as our measure a commodity, produced under the circumstances No. 1, the gold, for example, picked up by the hand, this will always purchase the same quantity of pure labour, and of such commodities as are produced by the same quantity of that labour; but it will not purchase the same quantity of commodities which come to need more or less of labour, nor the same quantity of the produce of hoarded labour, but less of it in proportion as wages rise, more as wages fall. Could we take as our measure a commodity produced under the circumstances No. 3, that is, by hoarded labour alone, it would always purchase the same quantity of the produce of hoarded labour, when no alteration had taken place in its productive powers, but less or more of the produce of immediate labour, according as profits, the wages of hoarded labour, rose or fell. A commodity, produced under the medium circumstances, answers the purpose best; because by far the greater number of commodities are produced under circumstances more nearly approaching to the medium than any of the extremes. Gold, therefore, which is produced in these circumstances, and with less variation in the quantity of the two kinds of labour applied to its production, than almost any other commodity, has this recommendation among others, to be the medium of exchange, that it is less imperfect as a measure of value than almost any other commodity, which could be taken. Such aberrations as are obvious, and capable of being in some degree foreseen, practical sagacity corrects by the proper allowances. This cannot be done when great and unexpected changes take place; and much disorder is the consequence.

SECTION IV.

OCCASIONS ON WHICH IT IS THE INTEREST OF
NATIONS TO EXCHANGE COMMODITIES WITH
ONE ANOTHER.

WE have already seen, that the benefits, derived
from the division and skilful distribution of labour,
form part of the motives which give rise to the exchange of commodities. Men will not confine themselves to the production of one only of the various
articles which contribute to the well-being of the
individual, unless they can, by its means, provide
themselves with others.

There is another circumstance, which very obviously affords a motive to exchange commodities.
Some can be produced only in particular places.
Metals, coals, and various other commodities of the
greatest importance, are the product of certain
spots. The same is the case with some vegetable
productions, to which every soil and climate are not
adapted. Certain commodities, though not confined
to particular spots, can yet be more conveniently and
cheaply produced in some places than in others;
commodities, for example, which require a great

consumption of fuel, in a coal country; commodities, the manufacture of which requires a strong moving power, where a sufficient fall of water can be obtained; commodities which require an extraordinary proportion of manual labour, where provisions, and consequently labour, are cheap.

These are all obvious causes. There is another cause, which requires rather more explanation. If two countries can both of them produce two commodities, corn, for example, and cloth, but not both commodities, with the same comparative facility, the two countries will find their advantage in confining themselves, each to one of the commodities, bartering for the other. If one of the countries can produce one of the commodities with peculiar advantages, and the other the other with peculiar advantages, the motive is immediately apparent which should induce each to confine itself to the commodity which it has peculiar advantages for producing. But the motive may no less exist, where one of the two countries has facilities superior to the other in producing both commodities.

By superior facilities, I mean, the power of producing the same effect with less labour. The conclusion, too, will be the same, whether we suppose the labour to be more or less highly paid. Suppose that Poland can produce corn and cloth with less labour than England, it will not follow that it may not be the interest of Poland to import one of the commodities from England. If the degree, in which it can produce with less labour, is the same in both cases ; if, for example, the same quantity of corn and cloth which Poland can produce, each with 100 days' labour, requires each 150 days' labour in England, Poland will have no motive to import either from England. But if, at the same time that the quantity of cloth, which, in Poland, is produced with 100 days' labour, can be produced in England with 150 days' labour ; the corn, which is produced in Poland with 100 days' labour, requires 200 days' labour in England ; in that case, it will be the interest of Poland to import her cloth from England. The evidence of these propositions may thus be traced.

If the cloth and the corn, each of which required 100 days' labour in Poland, required each 150 days' labour in England, it would follow, that the cloth of 150 days' labour in England, if sent to Poland, would be equal to the cloth of 100 days' labour in Poland : if exchanged for corn, therefore, it would exchange for the corn of only 100 days' labour. But the corn of 100 days' labour in Poland was supposed to be the same quantity with that of 150 days' labour in England. With 150 days' labour in cloth, therefore, England would only get as much corn in Poland as she could raise with 150 days' labour at home ; and she would, on importing it, have the cost of carriage besides. In these circumstances no exchange would take place.

If, on the other hand, while the cloth produced with 100 days' labour in Poland was produced with 150 days' labour in England, the corn which was produced in Poland with 100 days' labour could not be produced in England with less than 200 days' labour; an adequate motive to exchange would immediately arise. With a quantity of cloth which England produced with 150 days' labour, she would be able to purchase as much corn in Poland as was there produced with 100 days' labour; but the quantity, which was there produced with 100 days' labour, would be as great as the quantity produced in England with 200 days' labour. If the exchange, however, was made in this manner, the whole of the advantage would be on the part of England; and Poland would gain nothing, paying as much for the cloth she received from England, as the cost of producing it for herself.

But the power of Poland would be reciprocal. With a quantity of corn which cost her 100 days' labour, equal to the quantity produced in England by 200 days' labour, she could in the supposed case purchase, in England, the produce of 200 days' labour in cloth. The produce of 150 days' labour in England in the article of cloth would be equal to the produce of 100 days' labour in Poland. If, with the produce of 100 days' labour, she could purchase, not the produce of 150, but the produce of 200, she also would obtain the whole of the advantage, and England would purchase corn, which she could produce by 200 days' labour, with the product of as many days' labour in other commodities. The result of competition would be to divide the advantage equally between them.

Suppose the following case: That 10 yards of broad cloth purchase 15 yards of linen in England; and 20 yards in Germany. In exchanging 10 yards of English broad cloth for the equivalent of German linen, a saving, to the amount of 5 yards of linen, is the result of the bargain; and it is evident that the advantage will be shared upon the following principles. In England linen will fall, in relation to cloth, from the knowledge that 10 yards of cloth will purchase more than 15 yards of linen in Germany; and in Germany linen will rise as compared with cloth, from a knowledge that 20 yards of linen, if sent to England, will purchase more than 10 yards of cloth. It is the inevitable effect of such an interchange to bring the relative value of the two commodities to a level in the two countries; that is, to make the purchasing power of linen in respect to cloth, and of cloth in respect to linen, the same in both; bating the difference in the cost of carriage, each country paying the cost of the carriage of the commodity which it imports, and the value of that article being so much higher in the country which imports than in that which exports it.

To produce exchange, therefore, there must be two countries, and two commodities.

When both countries can produce both commodities, it is not greater absolute, but greater relative, facility, that induces one of them to confine itself to the production of one of the commodities, and to import the other.

When a country can either import a commodity, or produce it at home, it compares the cost of producing at home with the cost of procuring from abroad; if the latter cost is less than the first, it imports.

The cost at which a country can import from abroad depends, not upon the cost at which the foreign country produces the commodity, but upon what the commodity costs which it sends in exchange, compared with the cost which it must be at to produce the commodity in question, if it did not import it.

If a quarter of corn is produced in England with 50 days' labour, it may be equally her interest to import corn from Poland, whether it requires, in

Poland, 50 days' labour, or 60, or 40, or any other number. Her only consideration is, whether the commodity with which she can import a quarter costs her less than 50 days' labour.

Thus, if labour in Poland produce corn and cloth, in the ratio of eight yards to one quarter; but, in England, in the ratio of ten yards to one quarter, exchange will take place.

The practical conclusion may be commodiously and correctly stated thus:

Whenever the purchasing power of any commodity with respect to another is less, in one of two countries, than it is in the other, it is the interest of those countries to exchange these commodities with one another.

Unless the difference of purchasing power, which renders it the interest of nations to barter commodities with one another, be sufficiently great to cover the expense of carriage, and something more, no advantage is obtained.

SECTION V.

THE COMMODITIES IMPORTED ARE THE CAUSE OF THE BENEFITS DERIVED FROM A FOREIGN TRADE.

FROM what is stated in the preceding chapter, one general, or rather universal, proposition may be deduced. The benefit which is derived from exchanging one commodity for another, arises, in all cases, from the commodity *received*, not from the commodity given. When one country exchanges, in other words, when one country traffics with another, the whole of its advantage consists in the commodities *imported.* It benefits by the importation, and by nothing else.

This seems to be so very nearly a self-evident proposition, as to be hardly capable of being rendered more clear by illustration ; and yet it is so little in harmony with current and vulgar opinions, that it may not be easy by any illustration, to gain it admission into certain minds.

When a man possesses a certain commodity, he cannot benefit himself by giving it away. It seems to be implied, therefore, in the very fact of his parting with it for another commodity, that he is benefited by what he receives. His own commodity he might have kept, if it had been valued by him more than that for which he exchanges it. The fact of his choosing to have the other commodity rather than his own, is a proof that the other is to him more valuable than his own.

The corresponding facts are evidence equally conclusive in the case of nations. When one nation exchanges a part of its commodities for a part of the commodities of another nation, the nation can gain nothing by parting with its commodities; all the gain must consist in what it receives. If it be said that the gain consists in receiving money, it will presently appear, from the doctrine of money, that a nation derives no advantage, but the contrary, from possessing more than its due proportion of the precious metals.

In importing commodities which the country itself is competent to produce, as in the case, supposed above, of trade with Poland, we saw that England would import her corn from Poland, if she thus obtained, with the produce of so many days' labour in cloth, as much corn as it would have required a greater number of days' labour to produce in England. If it had so happened, that she could procure in Poland with the cloth, only as much corn as she could produce with the same quantity of labour at home, she would have had no advantage in the transaction. Her advantage would arise, not from what she should export, but wholly from what she should import.

The case in which a country imports commodities, which she herself is incompetent to produce, is of still more simple investigation. That country, or, more properly speaking, the people of that country, have certain commodities of their own, but these they are willing to give for certain commodities of other countries. They prefer having those other commodities. They are benefited, therefore, not by what they give away; that it would be absurd to say; but by what they receive.

SECTION VI.

CONVENIENCE OF A PARTICULAR COMMODITY, AS A MEDIUM OF EXCHANGE.

In exchanging commodities for one another directly, or in the way of barter, the wants of individuals could not be easily supplied. If a man had only sheep to dispose of; and wanted bread, or a coat; he might find himself subject to either of two difficulties: first, the man possessing the article which he wished to obtain, might be unwilling to accept of a sheep; or, secondly, the sheep might be of more value than the article which he wished to obtain, and could not be divided.

To obviate these difficulties, it would be fortunate if a commodity could be found, which every man, who had goods to dispose of, would be willing to receive, and which could be divided into such quantities, as would adapt themselves to the value of the articles which he wished to obtain. In this case, the man who had the sheep, and wanted bread or a coat, instead of offering his sheep to obtain them, would first exchange it for the equivalent quantity of this other commodity, and with that he would purchase the bread and other things for which he had occasion.

This, then, is the true idea of a medium of exchange. It is some one commodity, which, in order to effect an exchange between two other commodities, is first received in exchange for the one, and then given in exchange for the other.

Certain metals, gold, for example, and silver, were found to unite, in a superior degree, all the qualities desired in a medium of exchange. They were commodities which every man, who had goods to dispose of, was willing to receive in exchange. They could be divided into such portions as suited any quantity of other commodities which the purchaser desired to obtain. They possessed the further recommendation, by including a great value in a small bulk, of being very portable. They were also very indestructible; and less than almost any other commodities liable to fluctuations of value. From these causes, gold and silver have formed the principal medium of exchange in all parts of the globe.

The precious metals were liable to be mixed with baser metals in a manner which it was not easy to detect; and thus a less value was apt to be received than that which was understood to be so. It was also found inconvenient to perform the act of weighing every time that a purchase was to be made. An obvious expedient was calculated to remedy both inconveniences. Metal might be prepared of a determined fineness; it might be divided into portions

K

adapted to all sorts of purchases; and a stamp might be put upon it, denoting both its weight and its fineness. It is obvious, that the putting of this stamp could only be entrusted to an authority in which the people had confidence. The business has generally been undertaken by governments, and kept exclusively in their own hands. The business of putting the precious metals in the most convenient shape, for serving as the medium of exchange, has been denominated coining; and the pieces into which they are divided have obtained the appellation of money.

SECTION VII.

WHAT REGULATES THE VALUE OF MONEY.

By value of money, is here to be understood the proportion in which it exchanges for other commodities, or the quantity of it which exchanges for a certain quantity of other things.

It is not difficult to perceive, that it is the total quantity of the money in any country, which determines what portion of that quantity shall exchange for a certain portion of the goods or commodities of that country.

If we suppose that all the goods of the country are on one side, all the money on the other, and that they are exchanged at once against one another, it is obvious that one-tenth, or one-hundredth, or any other part of the goods, will exchange against one-tenth, or any part of the whole of the money; and that this tenth, &c. will be a great quantity or small, exactly in proportion as the whole quantity of the money in the country is great or small. If this were the state of the facts, therefore, it is evident that the value of money would depend wholly upon the quantity of it.

It will appear that the case is precisely the same in the actual state of the facts. The whole of the goods of a country are not exchanged at once against the whole of the money; the goods are exchanged in portions, often in very small portions, and at different times, during the course of the whole year. The same piece of money which is paid in one exchange to-day, may be paid in another exchange to-morrow. Some of the pieces will be employed in a great many exchanges, some in very few, and some, which happen to be hoarded, in none at all. There will, amid all these varieties, be a certain average number of exchanges, the same which, if all the pieces had performed an equal number, would have been performed by each; that average we may suppose to be any number we please; say, for example, ten. If each of the pieces of the money in the country perform ten purchases, that is exactly the same thing as if all the pieces were multiplied by ten, and performed only one purchase each. As each piece of the money is equal in value to that which it exchanges for, if each performs ten different exchanges to effect one exchange of all the goods, the value of all the goods in the country is equal to ten times the value of all the money.

If the quantity of money, instead of performing ten exchanges to exchange all the goods once, were ten times as great, and performed only one exchange, it is evident that whatever addition were made to the whole quantity, would produce a proportional diminution of value, in each of the minor quantities taken separately. As the quantity of goods, against which the money is all exchanged at once, is supposed to be the same, the value of all the money is no more, after the quantity is augmented, than before it was augmented. If it is supposed to be augmented one-tenth, the value of every part, that of an ounce for example, must be diminished one-tenth. Suppose the whole quantity 1,000,000 ounces, and augmented by one-tenth; the loss of value to the whole must be communicated proportionally to every part; but what one-tenth of a million is to a million, one-tenth of an ounce is to an ounce.

If the whole of the money is only one-tenth of the above supposed sum, and performs ten purchases in exchanging all the goods once, it of course exchanges each time against one-tenth of the goods. But if the tenth which exchanges against a tenth is increased in any proportion, it is the same thing as if the whole which exchanges against the whole were increased in that proportion. In whatever degree, therefore, the quantity of money is increased or diminished, other things remaining the same, in that same proportion, the value of the whole, and of every part, is reciprocally diminished or increased.

This, it is evident, is a proposition universally true. Whenever the value of money has either risen or fallen, (the quantity of goods, against which it is exchanged, and the rapidity of circulation, remaining the same,) the change must be owing to a corresponding diminution or increase of the quantity; and can be owing to nothing else. If the quantity of goods diminish, while the quantity of money remains unaltered, it is the same thing as if the quantity of money had been increased; and if the quantity of goods be increased, while the quantity of money remains unaltered, it is the same thing as if the quantity of money had been diminished.

Similar changes are produced by any alteration in the rapidity of circulation. By rapidity of circulation is meant, of course, the number of times the money must change hands to effect one sale of all the commodities.

The whole of the goods, which fall to be exchanged in the course of the year, is the amount contemplated in the above propositions. If there is any portion of the annual produce, which is not exchanged at all, as what is consumed by the producer; or which is not exchanged for money; any such portion is not taken into account, because what is not exchanged for money is in the same state, with respect to the money, as if it did not exist. If there is any part of what falls to be exchanged in the course of the year, which is exchanged two, or three, or more times, that also is not taken into account, because the effect is the same, with respect to the money, as if the goods had been increased to the amount of these multiplications, and exchanged only once.

SECTION VIII.

WHAT REGULATES THE QUANTITY OF MONEY.

WHEN we have ascertained, that quantity determines the value of money, we still have to inquire what it is that regulates quantity.

The quantity of money may seem, at first sight, to depend upon the will of the governments, which assume to themselves the privilege of making it, and may fabricate any quantity they please.

Money is made under two sets of circumstances; either when government leaves the increase or diminution of it free; or when it endeavours to control the quantity, making it great or small as it pleases.

When the increase or diminution of money is left free, government opens the mint to the public at large, making bullion into coins for as many as require it.

It is evident that individuals, possessed of bullion, will desire to convert it into coins, only when it is their interest to do so; that is, when their bullion, converted into coins, will be more valuable to them than in the shape of bullion.

This can only happen when the coins are peculiarly valuable, and when the same quantity of metal, in the state of coin, will exchange for more than in the state of bullion.

As the value of the coins depends upon the quantity of them, it is only when the quantity is to a certain degree limited, that they have this value. It is the interest of individuals, when coins are thus high in value, to carry bullion, to be coined; but by every addition to the number of the coins, the value of them is diminished; and at last the value of the metal in the coins, above the bullion, becomes too small to afford a motive for carrying bullion to be coined. If the quantity of money, therefore, should at any time be so small as to increase its value above that of the metal of which it is made, the interest of individuals operates immediately, in a state of freedom, to augment the quantity.

It is also possible for the quantity of money to be so large as to reduce the value of the metal in the coin, below its value in the state of bullion; in that case, the interest of individuals operates immediately to reduce the quantity. If a man has possessed himself of a quantity of the coins, containing, we shall say, an ounce of the metal, and if these coins are of less value than the metal in bullion, he has direct motive to melt the coins, and convert them into bullion : and this motive continues to operate till by the reduction of the quantity of money, the value of the metal in that state is so nearly the same with its value in bullion, as not to afford a motive for melting.

Whenever the coining of money, therefore, is free, its quantity is regulated by the value of the metal, it being the interest of individuals to increase or diminish the quantity, in proportion as the value of the metal in coins is greater or less than its value in bullion.

But if the quantity of money is determined by the value of the metal, it is still necessary to inquire what it is which determines the value of the metal. That is a question, however, which may be considered as already solved. Gold and silver are in reality commodities. They are commodities, for the attaining of which labour and capital must be employed. It is cost of production, therefore, which determines the value of these, as of other ordinary productions.

We have next to examine the effects which take place by the attempts of government to control the increase or diminution of money, and to fix the quantity as it pleases. When it endeavours to keep the quantity of money less than it would be, if things were left in freedom, it raises the value of the metal in the coin, and renders it the interest of every body, who can, to convert his bullion into money. By supposition, the government will not so convert it. He must, therefore, have recourse to private coining. This the government must, if it perseveres, prevent by punishment. On the other hand, were it the object of government to keep the quantity of money greater than it would be, if left in freedom, it would reduce the value of the metal in money, below its value in bullion, and make it the interest of every body to melt the coins. This, also, the government would have only one expedient for preventing, namely, punishment.

But the prospect of punishment will prevail over the prospect of profit, only if the profit is small. It is well known, that, where the temptation is considerable, private coinage goes on, in spite of the endeavours of government. As melting is a more easy process than coining, and can be performed more secretly, it will take place by a less temptation than coinage.

It thus appears, that the quantity of money is naturally regulated, in every country, by the value, in other words, by the productive cost, in that country, of the metals of which it is made ; that the government may, by forcible methods, reduce the actual quantity of money to a certain, but an inconsiderable extent, below that natural quantity; that it can also, but to a still less extent, raise it above that quantity.

When it diminishes the quantity below what it would be in a state of freedom, in other words, raises the value of the metal in the coins, above its value in bullion, it in reality imposes a seignorage. In practice, a seignorage is commonly imposed by issuing coins which contain rather less of the metal than they profess to contain, or less than that quantity to which they are intended to be an equivalent. By coining upon this principle, government makes a profit of the difference between the value of the metal in the coins, and that in bullion. Suppose the difference to be five per cent., the government obtains bullion at the market price, and makes it into coins which are worth five per cent. more than the bullion. Coins, however, will retain this value, only, if, as we have shown in the preceding section, they are limited in amount. To be able to limit them in amount, it is necessary that seignorage should not be so high as to compensate for the risk of counterfeiting; in short, that it should not greatly exceed the expense of coining.

SECTION IX.

THE EFFECT OF EMPLOYING TWO METALS BOTH AS STANDARD MONEY, AND OF USING SUBSIDIARY COINS, AT LESS THAN THE METALLIC VALUE.

SOME nations have made use of two metals, gold and silver, both, as standard money, or legal tender to any amount.

For this purpose it was necessary to fix a certain relative value between them. A certain weight of the one was taken to be equal in value to a certain weight of the other.

If the proportion thus fixed for the coins were accurately the proportion which obtained in the market, and continued so invariably, there would be no inconvenience in the two standards. The value of any sum would always be the same in either set of coins.

The relative value, however, of the two metals in the market is fluctuating.

Suppose that the value fixed for the coins is that of

15 to 1; in other words, that one piece of gold is equal to 15 pieces of silver of the same weight. A change takes place in the market, and this value becomes as 16 to 1. What follows?

A man who had a debt to pay, equal, let us say, to 100 of the gold pieces, or 1500 of the silver, finds it his interest to pay his debt not with gold. With his 100 pieces of gold he can go into the market and purchase as much silver as may be coined into 1600 pieces, with 1500 of which he may pay his debt, and retain 100 to himself. In this manner silver coins would be multiplied; and the quantity of the currency would be increased; its value would, therefore, be diminished; the gold in coins would thus become of less value than in bullion; hence the gold coins would be melted and would disappear.

After a fluctuation in one direction, it may take place in another. Silver may rise, instead of falling, as compared with gold. The relative value may become as 14 to 1. In this case it would be the interest of every man to pay in gold, rather than silver; and in this case it would be the silver coins which would disappear.

Two inconveniences are therefore incurred by the double standard. First, the value of the currency, instead of being rendered as steady in value as possible, is subjected to a particular cause of variation.

And, secondly, the country is put to the expence of a new coinage, as often as a change takes place in the relative value of the metals.

The case would be exactly the same, if a seignorage existed. Suppose that 10 per cent. were imposed as seignorage; it would be equally true, that the 100 pieces of gold; were the proportion changed, from 15 to 1, to 16 to 1; would purchase as much silver as would be exchanged at the mint for 1600 pieces of silver. While the market value of the two metals was the same as the mint value, one piece of gold purchased not only as much silver as was contained in 15 pieces of silver, but one-tenth more; after the change which we have just supposed, it purchases in the proportion of 16 to 15, that is, as much as will be contained in 16 pieces, and a tenth more.

The use of silver coins, for the purpose of small payments, or change, as it is called, of the more valuable coins, if they are legal tender only to a small amount, is not liable to the objections which apply to a double standard.

It has, indeed, been affirmed, that if they are issued, at a higher value than that of the metal contained in them, they will occasion the exportation of the gold coins. But it is easy to see that this is a mistake.

Suppose that our silver coins in this country are

10 per cent. above the value of the metal, but legal tender only to the extent of 40 shillings; every man, it is affirmed, has hence an interest in sending gold to Paris to buy silver.

The relative value of gold to silver in Paris and England is naturally pretty nearly the same; let us say as 15 to 1. An ounce of gold, therefore, will in Paris purchase 15 oz. of silver. But so it will in England. Where then is the advantage in going to France to purchase it?

You propose to coin it because it is 10 per cent. more valuable as coin.

But 10 per cent. of it is taken from you, and hence to you the advantage of the high value is lost.

Your silver coins with 10 per cent. added to them, would make the coins of full weight.

Suppose the price of silver to have sunk below the mint proportion, it would then be your interest to pay in silver if you could; but you can only pay to the extent of 40 shillings; it is therefore worth nobody's while to surcharge the market.

Besides, government reserves to itself the right of refusing to coin silver, when it pleases; it can therefore retain it of a high value.

Subsidiary coins cannot send the standard coins out of the country, unless the increased amount of them sink the value of the currency. The standard coins will not go in preference to bullion, unless they can be purchased cheaper than bullion.

SECTION X.

SUBSTITUTES FOR MONEY.

THE only substitute for money, of sufficient importance to require explanation, in this epitome of the science, is that species of written obligation to pay a sum of money, which has obtained the appellation of paper money.

The use of this species of obligation, as a substitute for money, seems to have originated in the invention of bills of exchange, ascribed to the Jews, in the feudal and barbarous ages.

When two countries, as England and Holland, traded with one another; when England, for example, imported Dutch goods, and Holland imported English goods, the question immediately arose, how payment was to be made for them. If England was under the necessity of sending gold and silver for the goods which she had brought from Holland, the expense was considerable. If Holland was under the necessity of sending gold and silver to England, the expense was also considerable. It was very obvious, however, that if there were two individuals, one of whom owed to the other 100*l*., and the other to him 100*l*., instead of the first man's taking the trouble to count down 100*l*. to the second, and the second man's taking the same trouble to count down 100*l*. to the first, all they had to do was to exchange their mutual obligations. The case was the same between England and Holland. If England had to pay a million of money to Holland, and had an equal sum to receive from Holland, instead of sending the money from England to Holland, it would save expence and trouble to consign to her creditors, in Holland, the money due to her in Holland; and those merchants in Holland, who owed money to England, and must have been at the expense of sending it, would be well pleased to be saved from that expense, by obeying an order to pay, in Holland, what they owed to a merchant in England. A bill of exchange was, literally, such an order. The merchant in England wrote to the merchant in Holland, who owed him a sum of money, " Pay to such and such a person, such and such a sum ;" and this was called drawing a bill upon that person. The merchants in Holland acted in the same manner, with respect to the persons in England, from whom they had money to receive, and to whom they had money to pay. When it so happened, that the money, which the two countries owed to one another, was equal, the payments balanced one another, and each country paid for the goods, which it had received, free, altogether, from the expense of transmitting money. Even when it happened that one of the two owed more than it had to receive, it had only the balance to discharge, and was relieved from all the rest of the expense.

The advantage, therefore, derived from the invention and use of bills of exchange, was very considerable. The use of them was recommended by a still stronger necessity, at the period of the invention, because the coarse policy of those times prohibited the exportation of the precious metals, and punished with the greatest severity any infringement of that barbarous law.

Bills of exchange not only served the purpose of discharging debts between country and country, but very often acted as a substitute for money, in the country to which they were sent. When a bill was drawn, payable after a certain time, the merchant to whom it was sent, if he had a debt to pay, or purchase to make, without having money ready for the purpose, paid with the bill, instead of money. One of these bills would often pass through several hands, and be the medium of payment in a number of transactions, before it was finally discharged by the person on whom it was drawn. To this extent, it performed the precise functions of paper money, and led the way to the further use of that important substitute.

As soon as it was discovered, that the obligation of a merchant of credit, to pay a sum of money, was, from the assurance that it would be paid as soon as demanded, considered of equal value with the money itself, and was without difficulty received in exchanges, as the money itself would have been received, there was motive sufficient to extend the use of the substitute. Those persons who had been accustomed to perform the functions of bankers in keeping the money of individuals, and exchanging against one another the coins of different countries, were the first who issued promises to pay certain sums of money, in the expectation that they would operate, as substitutes for money, in the business of purchase and sale. As soon as the use of such a substitute for money has begun, nothing is wanting but freedom, and the confidence of the public in the written promises, to enable the paper to supersede the use of the metal, and operate, almost exclusively, as the medium of exchange.

It remains to inquire what are the advantages derived from the use of this substitute; and what are the inconveniences to which it is liable.

SECTION XI.

ADVANTAGES DERIVED FROM THE USE OF PAPER MONEY.

THE precious metals, which are necessary to perform the functions of a medium of exchange, are bought with the commodities of the country. Manufactures, and the produce of the land, are exported ; and instead of other commodities, to be turned to use, gold and silver, to be employed as the medium of exchange, are imported for them. The value of the gold and silver, when they alone perform the business of exchange, always bears a considerable proportion,—in countries but little advanced in the arts of exchange, a large proportion, to the whole of the annual produce of the country. If each piece performs a hundred purchases in once exchanging the goods which fall to be exchanged in a year, the value of the money required is equal to a hundredth part of the whole of such goods, which, though not exactly corresponding with the annual produce, correspond with it so nearly, that we need not scruple to speak of them under that name. In countries in which money does not pass rapidly from hand to hand, it may be equal to a tenth of the whole of the annual produce.

It is evident that whatsoever part of the national property goes to provide the medium of exchange, is wholly inoperative with regard to production. Nothing produces, but the immediate instruments of production; the food of the labourer, the tools or machinery with which he labours, and the raw material, which he fabricates. If the whole, therefore, of the national property, which goes in this manner to provide a medium of exchange, equal to one-tenth, or one-hundredth part of the annual produce, could be taken from that employment, and converted into food, tools, and the materials of production, the productive powers of the country would receive a corresponding increase.

If it be considered, that the annual produce is equal, not only to the whole of the net revenue of the country, but, along with this, to the whole of the capital, excepting the part which is fixed in durable machinery, it may be easily understood how vast an accession is made to the means of production, by providing a substitute for the precious metals, as a medium of exchange.

Paper is also far more convenient, as a medium of exchange. A large sum in the shape of gold or silver is a cumbrous commodity. In performing exchanges of considerable value, the very counting of gold and silver is a tedious operation. By means of a bank note, the largest sum is paid as quickly as the smallest.

SECTION XII.

INCONVENIENCES TO WHICH THE USE OF PAPER MONEY IS LIABLE.

THE inconveniences to which paper money is liable, seem all to be comprehended under three heads.

First,—The failure of the parties, by whom the notes are issued, to fulfil their engagements.

Secondly,—Forgery.

Thirdly,—The alteration of the value of the currency.

1. The failure of the parties, by whom notes are issued, is an evil against which, under good institutions, the most powerful securities are spontaneously provided.

If competition were allowed to operate freely, and if no restriction were imposed on the number of the partners, who might be engaged in a bank, the business of banking, and of issuing notes, would naturally place itself on a footing, which would render paper currency very secure.

The number of banks would of course be multiplied; and no one bank would be able to fill with its circulation more than a certain district.

As little risk, where the partners were numerous, would be incurred by each of them, as the profits would be very sure, and the importance of having a good currency would be sensibly felt; there would be motive sufficient, to all the principal noblemen and gentlemen of the county, or other district, to hold shares in the local bank, and add to the security of the public.

In competition with such an establishment, any bank, of doubtful credit, would vainly endeavour to introduce its notes into circulation. The sense of interest keeps the attention sufficiently awake, and where education and knowledge are tolerably advanced, and the press is free, intellect is not wanting to guide the most ignorant to the proper conclusions. The people may be trusted to reject the notes of a suspected party, when they may have those of a party in whom they confide.

Another great advantage is gained, by the scheme of numerous banks, each supplying, under the safeguard of freedom and competition, a limited district; that if one of them fails, the evil is limited, and produces inconvenience to but a small portion of the community.

The interest, also, which banks, where numerous, have in supplanting one another, places them on the watch to discover any symptom of deficiency on the part of a rival; and each of them, knowing that it is vigilantly watched, is careful to avoid any fault, which can lead to a diminution of its credit.

In Scotland, where banking is nearly placed upon this desirable footing, and where paper money spontaneously filled the channels of circulation, long before the suspension of cash payments at the Bank of England, there have been few failures in the numerous banks which issued paper, notwithstanding all the fluctuations in the value of money, produced by that suspension, and all the convulsions of credit of which those fluctuations were the cause.

Such are the securities which the interest and intelligence of the parties would provide, without the intervention of the legislature. Of the securities which might be provided by the legislature, the following are among those which most obviously present themselves.

It might be rendered imperative upon every bank to transmit to some organ of government two monthly statements, one of the amount of its notes, another of the securities with which it was provided to meet the demands to which it was liable; while appropriate powers might be granted, for taking the necessary steps to protect the public, where proper securities might appear to be wanting.

As a great profit attends the issuing of notes in favourable circumstances, it is desirable that the benefit, if unattended with preponderant evil, should accrue to the public. The profit, it is observable, arising from the interest upon the notes as they are lent, is altogether distinct from the other benefit, arising from the conversion of a costly medium of exchange into instruments of production.

The issuing of notes is one of that small number of businesses, which it suits a government to conduct ; a business which may be reduced to a strict routine, and falls within the compass of a small number of clear and definite rules. If the public were its own banker, as it could not fail in payments to itself, the evils, liable to arise from the failure of the parties who issue notes to fulfil their engagements, could not possibly have place. The people, in this case, would provide the funds to fulfill the engagements, and the people would receive them. Political Economy does not contemplate the misapplication of the funds provided by the people. The cases of national bankruptcy, and of the non-payment of a government paper, by which the people of various countries have suffered, have all been cases in which the Many have been plundered for the benefit of the Few. When the people, as a body, are to receive the payment, which the people, as a body, provide the funds to make, it would be absurd to speak of their loss by a failure.

The chance of evil, then, from a failure in discharging the obligations contracted by the issue of paper money, is capable of being so much reduced, as to constitute no valid objection against an expedient, the benefits of which are great and indisputable. There are persons, however, who say, that if the benefits derived from paper money did surpass the chance of evil in quiet and orderly times, the case is very different in those of civil war or foreign invasion.

Civil war, and foreign invasion, are words which raise up vague conceptions of danger; and vague conceptions of danger are too apt to exert undue influence on the understanding.

In the first place, there is, in the present state of the civilised world, so little chance of civil war, or foreign invasion, in any country having a good government, and a considerable population, that, in contriving the means of national felicity, small allowance can be rationally required for it. To adopt a course of action, disadvantageous at all but times of civil war and foreign invasion, only because it were good on those occasions, would be as absurd, as it would be, in medicine, to confine all men continually to that species of regimen which suits a violent disease. If the advantages, which arise from the use of paper money, are enjoyed, without any considerable abatement, at all times, excepting those of civil war and foreign invasion, the utility of paper money is sufficiently proved.

To save ourselves from the delusion which vague conceptions of danger are apt to create, it is proper to inquire, what are the precise evils which may arise from paper money, during those rare and extraordinary times.

A civil war, or a foreign invasion, is attended with a great derangement of the circulating medium, when it is composed of gold and silver. At such a period there is a general disposition to hoard : a considerable proportion, therefore, of the medium of exchange is withdrawn from circulation, and the evils of a scarcity of money are immediately felt ; the prices of commodities fall ; the value of money rises ; those who have goods to sell, and those who have debts to pay, are subject to losses ; and calamity is widely diffused.

From the evils of hoarding, the community would be, in a great measure, secured, by the prevalence of paper money. And there are many reasons which may draw us to conclude, that those arising from the diminution of credit would be very little to be feared.

If the paper were issued by a government, which deserved the confidence of the people, a foreign invasion, which would concentrate the affections of the people towards the government, would not destroy the credit of its notes.

It would not be the interest of the invaders to destroy their credit, even in that part of the country, of which they might be in possession; because it would not be their interest to impair its productive powers.

Nobody would lose, ultimately; because, even if the circulation of the notes were prevented in the districts possessed by the enemy, they would recover their value the moment the enemy were expelled.

The effects would not be very different, if the circulation were provided by a well-conducted system of private banking. It would be the interest of all parties to preserve the circulating medium in credit. It would be the interest of the enemy to preserve it in the districts which he possessed. At most, he could only prevent the circulation for a time; for, after his expulsion, the notes would be redeemed; either by the responsible parties who had issued them; or, if they had lost their property through the operations of the enemy, out of the compensation money which the government would allow.

It is not probable, that, even in a civil war, any

considerable discredit should attend a well-established paper currency. The country is, of course, divided between the hostile parties, in portions more or less nearly equal. It is evidently not the interest of the government, in that part of the country which it commands, to discredit the paper currency, whether it had been issued by itself, or by private bankers. As little is it the interest of the opposite party, to do any thing which shall disorder the regularity of transactions, in that part of the country, where it governs, and from which all its means of prevailing over its opponents must be drawn. If the circulating medium consists of the notes of private bankers, situated within that part of the country, it is the interest, on a double account, of the party to protect them. It is its interest to protect them, even if they are paper of the government. For whom would it injure, as the holders of them, but its own people? Whose business would it disturb by the want of a circulating medium, but the people upon whose means and affections it wholly depends? By protecting the paper of the government, it makes it, in reality, its own.

Experience is in favour of all these conclusions; since it has been repeatedly found, that the presence of hostile armies, and even internal commotions, have occasioned little disturbance to a paper currency, the value of which was but tolerably secured.

2. Forgery, to which bank notes are exposed, is an

evil of the same sort as counterfeiting. This, though an evil of great magnitude, under so imperfect a system of banking as that, which is created by the existence of a great monopolizing establishment, like the Bank of England, would, under such a system of banking, as that which we have been just contemplating, be inconsiderable. Where one great bank supplies the circulation of a great part of the country, there is opportunity for the circulation of a great amount of forged notes, and motive to incur both a great risk and a great expense. But if every bank supplied only a small district, a small amount of the forged notes of such a bank could find their way into the circulation. Banks, too, which are subject to the useful principle of competition, are afraid to discredit their own notes and render the people shy of taking them, by refusing payment of such as are forged ; they rather choose to pay them in silence, to detect as well as they can the authors of the forgery, and circumscribe its amount. In this manner individuals severally are exempted from loss ; and if a loss is willingly sustained by the banks, it is only because they find compensation.

3. The last of the three inconveniences, liable to arise from the use of paper money, is an alteration in the value of the currency.

This alteration is always an act of the government; and is not peculiar to paper money.

We have already seen, that the value of a metallic currency is determined by the value of the metal which it contains. That of a paper currency, therefore, exchangeable at pleasure, either for coins or for bullion, is also determined by the value of the metal which can be obtained for it. The reason is obvious. If the paper should at any time be reduced below the value of the metal, every person who held a bank note, the less valuable commodity, would demand for it the more valuable commodity, the metal. If the promise were, as in England, to pay an ounce of gold for 3*l.* 17*s.* 10½*d.* of paper, it would be the interest of the holders of the notes to demand gold in exchange, the moment 3*l.* 17*s.* 10½*d.* in paper became of less value than an ounce of gold; that is, the moment gold rose above the mint price.

But, in these circumstances, it would be the interest of those who issued the notes to raise their value by reducing their quantity. If they endeavoured to maintain the high quantity, they would be condemned perpetually to issue and perpetually to withdraw; because every man who became possessed of any of their notes would have an interest in bringing them back again for gold; and on each of these occasions the issuers would sustain a loss. They would issue the notes at the rate of 3*l.* 17*s.* 10½*d.*; that is they would receive a value of 3*l.* 17*s.* 10½*d.* when they issued them; but when they received them

M

back, they would be obliged to pay an ounce of gold, for 3*l.* 17*s.* 10½*d.* of their notes; and that ounce might cost them 4*l.*, or any greater sum.

If the currency were supplied by paper, without coins, the issuers of the paper could, by lessening its quantity, and thereby enhancing its value, reduce the price of gold.   Suppose, by this means, they were to reduce it to 3*l.* per ounce.   They might fill their coffers with gold at this price; and having done so, they might raise its price by increasing their issues till it became the interest of the holders of their notes to demand it of them at 3*l.* 17*s.* 10½*d.*   They would make a profit of 17*s.* 10½*d.* on every ounce of gold thus trafficked; and they might continually re-peat the operation.   A simple expedient, however, would be an effectual security against this danger. As the obligation to sell gold at a fixed price renders it the interest of those who issue paper not to in-crease their notes in such a manner as to raise gold above that price, so an obligation on them to buy gold at a fixed price would render it their interest not to reduce the amount of their notes in such a manner as to sink it below that price.   The value of the notes might thus be kept very steadily conform-able to that of the metallic standard.

In the case of a metallic currency, government can reduce the value of the coins, only by lessening the quantity of the precious metal contained in them;

otherwise, as soon as it reduced the value of the coins sufficiently to afford a motive for melting them, they would, as fast as issued, disappear. In the case of a paper currency, it is only necessary for government to withdraw the obligation to pay metal for it on demand, when the quantity may be increased, and thereby the value diminished, to any amount.

Paper currency is issued without obligation to pay for it, in two ways : either, when government is the issuer, and renders its paper legal tender, without obligation to give metal for it in exchange ; or when the paper currency is regulated by one great establishment, as the Bank of England, and government suspends its obligation to pay for its notes.

The effects of an increase of the quantity, and consequent diminution of the value of the currency in any particular country, are two : first, a rise of prices ; secondly, a loss to all those persons who had a right to receive a certain sum of money of the old and undiminished value.

By the term *price*, I always understand the quantity of money which is given in exchange. An alteration in the value of money, it is obvious, alters the relative value of nothing else. All things —bread, cloth, shoes, &c. rise in value as compared with money ; but not one of them rises in value as compared with any other.

This difference of price is, in itself, of no consequence to any body.   The man who has goods to sell
gets more money for them, indeed; but this money
will purchase him just the same quantity of commodities, as he was enabled to purchase with the price
he obtained before.   The man who has goods to
purchase has more money to give for them ; but he is
enabled to do so, by getting just as much more for
the commodities he has to sell.

With respect to the second effect of a degradation
in the value of money, it is to be observed, that there
exists at all times, in civilized countries, a number of
obligations to pay certain sums of money to individuals : either all at once, as debts ; or in succession,
as annuities.   It is very obvious, that the individual
who has contracted with a man to receive 100*l.* sustains a loss when the currency is reduced in value
and he receives no more than 100*l.*   It is equally
obvious that the party who has to pay the sum, is
benefitted to the same amount.   These circumstances
are reversed when the alteration which has taken
place is an increase of the value.   In that case the
man who has to pay sustains the loss ; the man who
receives payment makes the gain.   These losses are
evils of great magnitude, as far as men's feelings and
happiness are concerned ; and they imply a gross
violation of those rules for the guardianship of that
happiness, which are comprehended under the term

justice. It is, however, no destruction, and consequently no loss, of property.

Hume has supposed that certain other effects are produced by the increase of the quantity of money. When an augmentation of money commences, individuals, more or fewer, go into the market with greater sums. The consequence is, that they offer better prices; and Hume affirms, that the increased prices give encouragement to producers, who are incited to greater activity and industry, and that an increase of production is the consequence.

This doctrine implies a want of clear ideas respecting production. The agents of production are the commodities themselves, not the price of them. They are the food of the labourer, the tools and machinery with which he works, and the raw materials which he works upon. These are not increased by the increase of money: how then can there be more production? This is a demonstration that the conclusion of Hume is erroneous. It may be satisfactory also to unravel the fallacy of his argument.

The man who goes first to market with the augmented quantity of money, either raises the price of the commodities which he purchases, or he does not.

If not, he gives no additional encouragement to

production. The supposition, therefore, must be, that he does raise prices. But exactly in proportion as he raises prices, he sinks the value of money. He therefore gives no additional encouragement to production.

It will perhaps be said, by a persevering objector, that the man who first goes to market with the additional quantity of money, raises the price of the commodities which he immediately purchases : that the producers of those commodities are therefore encouraged to greater industry, because the price of other commodities, namely, of all those which they have occasion to purchase, has not risen. But this he is not allowed to say. The first man who came with an additional quantity of money into the market to purchase the commodities of those producers, raised the price of those commodities. And why? Because he came with an additional quantity of money. They go into the market to purchase another set of commodities, and go with an additional quantity of money. They raise, therefore, the price of those commodities. And in this manner the succession goes on. Of all those commodities with which no additional quantity of money has yet come in contact the price remains unaltered. The moment an additional quantity of money comes in contact with them, the price is proportionally raised.

The whole of the business of any country may be

considered as practically divided into a great number of little markets, some in one place, some in another, some of one sort of commodity, some of another: the money, of course, distributed proportionally among them. Into each of these markets, in the ordinary state of things, there comes, on the one side, a certain quantity of commodities; on the other side a certain quantity of money; and the one is exchanged against the other. Wherever any addition takes place in the quantity of goods, without any addition to the quantity of money, the price falls, and of necessity in the exact proportion of the addition which has been made. If this is not clear to every apprehension already, it may be rendered palpable by adducing a simple case. Suppose the market to be a very narrow one; of bread solely, on the one side; and money on the other. Suppose that the ordinary state of the market is 100 loaves on the one side, and 100 shillings on the other; the price of bread, accordingly, a shilling a loaf. Suppose, in these circumstances, that the quantity of loaves is increased to 200, while the money remains the same: it is obvious that the price of the bread must fall one half, or to six-pence per loaf. It would not be argument to say, that part of the bread would not be sold, but taken away unsold. If it is taken away unsold, it is the same thing, with respect to the market, as if it had never been brought. These conclusions, with respect to an increase in the quantity of commodities, no man disputes.   Is it not obvious that the some conclusions are true with respect to an increase in the quantity of the opposite commodity—the money ?

All the consequences, therefore, of altering the value of money, whether by raising or depressing it, are injurious.   There is no security, however, against it, as it is a deed of government, but that which is the sole security against the misdeeds of government ; its dependence upon the people.   The obligation of paying the notes in the metal is a necessary security, where they are issued at pleasure by private bankers.   If they were issued by a government strictly responsible to the people, it would not be indispensible ; for in that case the utility of keeping gold at the mint price, or, in other words, the currency of the same value as if it was metallic, might be so distinctly understood, that it would not be the interest of those intrusted with the powers of government to allow it to vary.

We have already seen, in treating of the properties which recommended the precious metals for the instrument of exchange, that they are less than almost any other commodity subject to fluctuation of value.   They are not, however, exempt from changes, partly temporary, and partly permanent.   The permanent changes take place, chiefly in consequence of a change in the cost of procuring them.   The greatest change of this kind, recorded in history, is that which took place on the discovery of the mines of America, from which, with the same quantity of labour a greater quantity of the metals was obtained. The temporary changes take place, like the temporary changes in the value of other commodities, by a derangement of the balance of demand and supply. For the payment of troops in a foreign country, or subsidies to foreign governments and other operations, a great quantity of gold or silver is sometimes bought up, and sent out of the country. This enhances the price, till the balance is restored by importation. The profit which may be acquired operates immediately as a motive to restore it. In the interval, however, an advantage may be derived from a paper money not convertible immediately into the metals. If convertible, gold will be demanded, paper will be diminished, and the value of the currency will be raised. If not convertible, the currency may be retained of the same, or nearly the same value as it was before. This, indeed, can scarcely be done, and the remedy applied with safety, unless where the whole is paper, and government has the supply in its own hands. In that case the sameness in the quantity of the currency, as it would be perfectly known, would be a sufficient index and security. If the price of gold rose suddenly above the mint price, or, in other words, above the rate of the bank notes, without any alteration in the quantity of the currency, the sameness in the quantity of currency would be a sufficient

index that the rise was owing to a sudden absorption
of the gold; which, after a time, would return.   If
in such circumstances the obligation of keeping up
the value of the paper to that of the gold were sus-
pended for a short time, a sufficient security against
any considerable alteration in the value of the currency would be found in the obligation of keeping
the quantity of it the same; because, during any
short period of time, there can be no such diminution
or increase of the quantity of business to be done by
it, as to require any material alteration.   That in
the hands of an irresponsible government such
power of suspension would be dangerous, is true.
But an irresponsible government involves all kinds
of danger, and this among the rest.

SECTION XIII.

THE VALUE OF THE PRECIOUS METALS IN EACH COUNTRY DETERMINES WHETHER IT SHALL EXPORT OR IMPORT.

METALLIC money, or more generally speaking, the precious metals, are nothing more, considered strictly, and in their essence, than that commodity which is the most generally bought and sold, whether by individuals, or by nations.

In ordinary language, it is immediately acknowledged, that those commodities alone can be exported, which are cheaper in the country from which, than in the country to which, they are sent; and that those commodities alone can be imported, which are dearer in the country to which, than in the country from which, they are sent.

According to this proposition, if gold is cheaper in any one country, as in England, for example, it will be exported from England. Again, if gold is dearer in England than in other countries, it will be imported into England. But, by the very force of the terms, it is implied, that in any country where gold is cheap, other commodities are dear. Gold is cheap, when a greater quantity of it is required to purchase commodities; and commodities are dear, for the same reason; namely, when a greater quantity of gold is required to purchase them. When the value of gold, therefore, in England, is low, gold will be exported from England, on the principle that all commodities which are free to seek a market, go from the place where they are cheap to the place where they are dear. But as, in the fact that gold is cheap, is implied the correlative and inseparable fact, that other commodities, at the same time, are dear, it follows, that, when gold is exported, less of other commodities can be exported; that no commodities can be exported, if the value of gold is so low as to raise the price of all of them above the price in other countries; and that a diminished quantity alone can be exported, if the value of gold is only reduced so far as to raise the price of some of them above the price in other countries.

It is evident, therefore, that a country will export commodities, other than the precious metals, only when the value of the precious metals is high. It is equally evident, that she will import, only when the value of the precious metals is low. The increase, therefore, of the quantity of the precious metals, which diminishes the value of them, gradually diminishes and tends to destroy the power of exporting other commodities; the diminution of the quantity of the precious metals which increases their value, increases, by a similar process, the motive to exportation of other commodities, and, of course, in a state of freedom, the quantity exported.

SECTION XIV.

THE VALUE OF THE PRECIOUS METAL, OR MEDIUM OF EXCHANGE, WHICH DETERMINES EXPORTATION, IS NOT THE SAME IN ALL COUNTRIES.

WHEN we speak of the value of the precious metal, we mean the quantity of other things for which it will exchange.

But it is well known that money is more valuable, that is, goes farther in the purchase of commodities, not only in one country than another, but in one part than another of the same country.

In some of the more distant places of Wales, for example, money is more valuable than in London; in common language, we say, that living is more cheap; in other words, commodities may be purchased with a smaller quantity of money: and this state of things is habitual, money having no tendency to go from London where its value is low, to increase its quantity in Wales where its value is high. This phenomenon requires explanation.

The fact is, that the whole of such difference as

is habitual, and has no tendency to produce a transit of the metals, resolves itself into cost of carriage. Corn, butchers'-meat, and other commodities, which are produced in Wales, are cheaper than in London, because the supply of London comes from a distance, and the original price is enhanced by cost of carriage. But as there are certain commodities which thus are cheaper in Wales than in London, so there are others which are cheaper in London than in Wales. Such are all the commodities which are either manufactured in London, or imported into London from abroad. Just as the corn and other commodities, which come from Wales to London, are enhanced by the cost of carriage; so those commodities which are sent from London to Wales, are dearer in Wales than in London, by the whole of the cost which is incurred in transporting them. The fact, therefore, is, that in Wales some commodities are cheaper, and some are dearer, than in London; but those which are cheaper are the articles of principal importance; they are the necessaries of life, the articles the consumption of which constitutes the principal part of almost every man's expenditure. What is more, they are the articles the money-value of which determines the money-value of labour; every thing which a man has done for him, therefore, is done cheaper than it is in London. And, lastly, the gross commodities, which are the produce of Wales, cost much more for carriage, in proportion to their value, than the fine commodities which are received from

London : the cost of the gross commodities in London is much more raised above the price of them in Wales, than the price of the fine commodities in Wales is raised above the price of them in London. The cost of living, therefore, is greater in London than in Wales, for this reason, solely, because people in London pay more for carriage. If the value of the metal in Wales rose ever so little above that limit, a profit equal to that rise would immediately operate as a motive for sending it to Wales.

From two places in the same country, let us transfer the consideration to two different countries. The cost of living is higher; in other words, the value of the precious metals is lower in England, than in Poland. The difference here, also, resolves itself wholly into the cost of carriage. Let us suppose that England receives a considerable portion of her supply of corn from Poland, and sends her the whole, or the greater part, of her fine manufactures : corn, it is evident, will be dearer in England ; but fine manufactures will be dearer in Poland. For the same reasons that money, as we have shown, goes farther in Wales, than in London, it is easy to see that it will, in this case, go farther in Poland than in England ; in other words, the value of gold in Poland will be greater than in England, just so much as to compensate for the greater cost of carriage which England sustains. The moment it rises above that value, a profit may be made by sending it to England.

SECTION XV.

MODE IN WHICH THE PRECIOUS METAL, OR
MEDIUM OF EXCHANGE, DISTRIBUTES ITSELF
AMONG THE NATIONS OF THE GLOBE.

In the country of the mines, whence gold distributes itself to the rest of the world, gold is in relative plenty. As an addition is constantly making to the quantity already possessed, there is a constant tendency in the gold of that country to fall in relative value; in other words, a constant tendency in the price of other things to rise. As soon as any commodities have risen sufficiently high to enable them to be imported, they will come in from that country, be it what it may, from which, prime cost and cost of carriage taken together, they come the cheapest; and gold will go out in exchange.

By this importation of gold into that second country, it becomes relatively plentiful there, and prices rise. Some commodity, or commodities, become there at last so dear, that they can be imported, with profit, from another country : commodities, as in the previous instance, come in, and gold goes out. It is unnecessary to trace the operation farther. In this manner gold proceeds from country to country,

N

through the whole connected chain of the commercial world.

In a preceding section we found, that it is the interest of two nations to exchange with one another two sorts of commodities, as often as the relative cost of producing them is different in the two countries. If four quarters of corn, for example, and 20 yards of cloth, cost, each, the same quantity of labour in England, but not the same quantity in Poland, it would be the interest of the two countries, the one to produce corn, the other to produce cloth, and to exchange them with one another.

Suppose, while four quarters of corn and 20 yards of cloth required the same quantity of labour in England; that in Poland 20 yards of cloth required twice as much labour as four quarters of corn. In these circumstances, cloth, as compared with corn, would be twice as dear in Poland as in England; in other words, four quarters of corn, which in England would be of equal value with 20 yards of cloth, would in Poland be equal to no more than 10 yards. In a traffic of these commodities, between England and Poland, there would be a value of 5 yards of cloth to be gained by each upon every repetition of the transaction.

Supposing, as we have done, that in Poland, if she produced corn and cloth for herself, four quarters of corn would have the same value as 10 yards of cloth, it follows, that if she had the use of money, the price of four quarters of corn, and of 10 yards of cloth, would be the same. In England, according to the supposition, the price of four quarters of corn and that of 20 yards of cloth would be the same.

There are two supposeable cases. The price of one of the two commodities, corn, for example, is either—1. equal in the two countries, or—2. it is not equal. The illustration of any one of these cases will suffice for both.

Let us suppose that, in the two countries, the price of corn is equal. If it is, the price of a yard of cloth must in Poland be twice as great as it is in England. In these circumstances, what will happen is obvious : the cloth, which is cheap in England, will go to Poland, where it is dear; and there it will be sold for gold, because there can be no counter impor-tation of corn, which, by supposition, is already as cheap in England as in Poland.

By the importation, in this manner, of English cloth into Poland, gold goes out of Poland, and comes into England. The consequence is, that gold becomes more plentiful in England, less plentiful in Poland. From this first consequence, a second ensues ; that prices gradually rise in England, fall in Poland : the price of corn, for example, and, along

with it, the price of cloth, rise in England, fall in
Poland.   If when we suppose the traffic to begin, the
price of corn in each country is 1*l.* per quarter, the
price of cloth being, by consequence, in Poland 8*s.*,
in England 4*s.* per yard; the supposed exchange of
cloth for gold will gradually, in England, raise the
price of corn above, in Poland sink it below, 1*l.* per
quarter; raise the price of cloth in England above
4*s.* per yard, sink it below 8*s.* per yard in Poland.
In this manner, the price of corn in the two countries
gradually recedes from equality, the price of cloth
gradually approaches it.   At a certain point in this
progress, corn becomes so dear in England, and cheap
in Poland, that the difference of price will pay for the
cost of carriage.   At that moment a motive arises for
the importation of corn into England; and prices
regulate themselves in such a manner, that in England corn is dearer than in Poland, by the expense of
carrying corn; cloth is dearer in Poland than in England, by the expense of carrying cloth, from the one
country to the other.   At this point, the value of the
cloth imported into the one country, and that of the
corn imported into the other, balance one another.
The exchange is then at par, and gold ceases to
pass.

From the consideration of the same circumstances,
it will farther be seen, that no alteration can take
place in the interchange of commodities between the
two countries, without a new distribution of the pre-

cious metal; that is, a change in the relative quantities which they previously possessed.

Let us suppose that, in England, some new commodity is produced, which Poland desires to obtain. A quantity of this commodity is imported into Poland; and it can be paid for only in gold, because we have supposed that at this time, the corn and cloth, respectively imported, pay for one another. In this case, as in that which I have previously explained, the price of commodities soon begins to rise in England, fall in Poland. In proportion as prices rise in England, and fall in Poland, a motive is produced to import a greater quantity of Polish goods into England, a less quantity of English goods into Poland. And again the balance is restored.

SECTION XVI.

MONEY TRANSACTIONS BETWEEN NATIONS—
BILLS OF EXCHANGE.

THE moneys of different countries are different; that is to say, they consist of different portions of the precious metals, and go by different names. The pound sterling, for example, is the money of England, the dollar is the money of certain other countries; the pound sterling contains one quantity of the precious metal, the dollar contains a less quantity; and so of other varieties.

The purchases which are made by one country in another country, are, like other purchases, made by money. If the Dutch merchant, for example, purchase goods in England, he buys them at so many pounds sterling. If the English merchant buys goods in Holland, he buys them at so many guilders. To pay the pound sterling, the Dutch merchant must either send the English money, or an equivalent. The direct equivalent is a quantity of the precious metal equal to what is contained in the pounds sterling due. If the Dutch merchant has no other medium but guilders, he must send as many guilders as contain an equal quantity of the precious metals.

When the language now used by the merchants of Europe was established, a computation was made of the quantity of one currency which contained the same quantity of the precious metal, as a certain given quantity of another. This was called the par of exchange. The guilder contained not quite so much of the metal as two shillings English; but to simplify our language, let us suppose that it contained just as much. The par of exchange was then, 10 guilders to 1l.; or, in the abridged language of the merchants, 10.

The business of exchange, however, between country and country, is carried on, not by transmitting currency, or the metals, but, in a much greater degree, by the instrumentality of bills. The language, which the merchants have adopted for carrying on the traffic of bills, is very elliptical and abridged; and being, in several respects, not well chosen, is a source of obscurity and misapprehension.

The simple transaction is this. The merchant in London, to whom a merchant in Amsterdam owes a sum of money, writes a line to the merchant in Amsterdam, directing him to pay the money. The writing of this line is called drawing; the line itself is called a bill; and the person whom the line is written *to,* is said to be drawn *upon.* If the merchant in London, at the same time that he has money to receive from Amsterdam, has money to pay in Amsterdam, he draws his bill upon his debtor in Amsterdam, to the order of his creditor; or, in other words, his line written to the person who owes him money in Amsterdam, is a line directing him to pay the amount to that other person to whom he is indebted. If the sum to be received is equal to the sum to be paid, the bill discharges the debt; if it is less, it pays as far as it goes, and the difference constitutes a balance.

It so happens, in the course of business, that the individuals who import goods from Holland, for example, are not the same individuals who export goods to Holland. The merchants who import corn, or butter, or tallow, from Holland, are one set of merchants; the merchants who export cottons and hardware to Holland, are merchants of another description; the individuals, therefore, who have money to receive from Holland, have nothing to do with any payments in Holland; they make a demand for their money, and expect it shall be paid. There are other individuals, however, who have money to pay in Holland, and who, to save themselves the expense of sending money, are desirous of obtaining from the individuals, who have money to receive from Holland, orders upon their debtors, that is, bills drawn upon them for the sum. The English exporters, who have money to receive from Holland, therefore, draw bills, upon their correspondents in Holland, and, without needing to wait for the return from Holland, receive the money in England from the English importers.

There are thus two sets of persons in England: one, who have money to receive from Holland; another, who have money to send to Holland. They who have money to send, are desirous of meeting with the persons who have money to receive, and bills to draw; the persons, again, who have bills to draw, and money to receive, are desirous of meeting with the persons who have money to pay, and who would give it them immediately, and save them the delay of waiting the return from Holland. But these two sets of men do not always know how to find one another. This gives rise to a set of middle men, who, under the name of bill-brokers and exchange-brokers, perform the function of bringing them together, or rather act as the medium between them.

When it so happens that the amount, for which bills are drawn, is the same with that, for which bills are wanted; in other words, when those, who have money to receive abroad, are equal to those, who have money to pay; the amount of bills to be bought, and the amount to be sold, will be exactly the same. For each man desirous to purchase a bill on Holland, there will be another man, equally desirous to sell one. There will be neither premium, therefore, on the one side, nor discount on the other ; the bills, or in the language of the merchants, the exchange, will be at par.

When it happens, however, that the debts and credits are not equal; that England, for example, has more money to pay, than she has to receive; in other words, has imported to a greater amount than she has exported, there are more persons who want to purchase bills on Holland, than there are persons to sell them. Those who cannot obtain bills to discharge their debts in Holland must send the metals. That, however, is an operation, attended with a considerable cost.   There is, therefore, a competition for bills; and the merchants give for them rather more than they are worth.   A bill, for example, drawn on Holland, for 10,000 guilders, (the 10,000 guilders being, by supposition, equal to 1,000l.) will be willingly purchased for something more than 1,000l.   In this case, the exchange is said to be in favour of Holland, and against England. It is against England, because in Holland, when bills are drawn upon England, there are more people who have bills to sell, than people who have any occasion to buy.   There is a competition, therefore, among the people who wish to sell, and the price falls.   A bill on England for 1,000l., instead of selling for 10,000 guilders, will sell for something less.   This, it is evident, is a discouragement to the Dutch merchant who exports goods to England.

It is also a discouragement to the English merchant who imports goods from Holland, and who, in addition to the 10,000 guilders, which his goods have cost, must pay something more than 1000*l.*, or 10,000 guilders, for a bill to pay them. On the other hand, there is an encouragement to the English merchant, who exports goods to Holland, inasmuch as he receives for his bill of 10,000 guilders on Holland, rather more than 1,000*l.*, which is the value of his goods ; he is, therefore, stimulated, by this increase of profit, to increase the quantity of his trade.

It is very easy to see, what is the limit to this variation in the price of bills, called in the language of merchants, the exchange. The motive to the purchase of a bill is the obligation of paying a debt. The merchant, however, on whom it is incumbent to pay a debt in Holland, can pay it without a bill, by sending the metal. To send the metal is attended with a certain cost. If he can obtain the bill without paying beyond this cost, he will purchase the bill. This cost, therefore, is the utmost amount of the premium which he will pay for a bill, and the limit to the rise of its price. As the cost of sending the metal, which is a great value in a small bulk, is never considerable, the exchange can never vary from par to a considerable amount.

It is well known in commerce, how a balance is

transferred from one country to another, by means of bills of exchange.

If a balance is due by England to Holland, and by Hamburgh to England, the holder of a bill at Amsterdam for 1,000*l.* upon England, will not send his bill to England, where it will fetch him only 1,000*l.*; if by sending it to Hamburgh, it will fetch him something more; (i. e.) if he has a debt to pay at Hamburgh, when bills upon England are there at a premium, or if the premium will exceed the cost of transporting the gold from Hamburgh to Amsterdam. A debt, which England owed to Holland, is thus paid by a credit which it had at Hamburgh. In England, the merchants who have imported from Holland, pay for the goods which they have imported, by paying the merchants, who have exported to Hamburgh, for the goods which they have exported.

Such are the transactions between country and country, by means of bills of exchange; and such is the language in which they are expressed. There are two states of things, in which these operations take place: The First, when the currency of both countries remains the same as at the time when the par of exchange was originally computed; when 10 guilders of Holland, for example, contained as much of the precious metal as 1*l.* sterling; and the par of exchange, of course, was said to be 10: The Second, when the relative value of the two currencies does not remain the same; as, for example, when 1*l.*, instead of being equal to 10 guilders, becomes equal to 12, or to no more than 8.

If we suppose the quantity of the precious metal in the pound sterling to be diminished in such a degree, that it contains no greater quantity than that which is contained in 8 guilders, the par of exchange, in this case, would really be 8, instead of 10. The merchants, however, from the time at which the par of exchange appears to have been originally computed, never altered their language. If the par of exchange between the guilder and the pound sterling was 10, it continued to be called 10, though the relative value of the currencies might be changed; though the pound sterling, for example, might become equal to 8 guilders only, instead of 10. Notwithstanding this the value of the bills was regulated according to the real value of the currencies; a bill for so many pounds sterling was not when such a change took place equal to a bill for as many times 10 guilders, but for as many times 8. As the par of exchange, however, still was called 10, though really 8, the exchange was said to be against England, in the proportion of 10 to 8, or 20 per cent. This 20 per cent. of unfavourable exchange was altogether nominal; for when there was this 20 per cent. of discount on the English bill, the exchange was really at par. The language, therefore, was improper and deceptious; but if, in such case, it is borne in mind, that 20 per cent. against England means the same as par, it will then be easy to see that every thing which we demonstrated, in the preceding pages, as true with respect to the par, will, in this case, be true with respect to the 20 per cent. Every thing which raises the exchange above par, according to the proper language, makes it as much less than 20, according to the improper; every thing which reduces it below par, according to the proper, makes it as much more than 20, according to the improper. All the effects which follow from what is called the rise above, or fall below par, in the one case, follow from the same things, but called by different names, in the other. On this, therefore, I have no occasion to enlarge.

When the currencies of two countries are metallic, a change in their relative value beyond the fluctuations which are limited by the expense of transmiting the metals, and continually corrected by their transmission, can only happen by a change in the relative quantity of the metal they contain; there being checks, as we have already seen, which prevent any considerable difference between the value of a metallic currency and that of the metal which it contains There is, however, another case, namely, that of a paper money, not convertible into the metallic. This requires to be considered by itself.

Let us resume the former supposition, that the pound sterling contains as much of the precious metal as 10 guilders; and let us suppose that a paper money, not payable in the metals, is issued in England, in such quantity, that a pound in that money is reduced 20 per cent. below the value of the metal contained in a pound sterling; it is easy to see that a bill for 100*l*. sterling, in this case, is of the same value exactly as a bill for 100*l*. sterling when the currency was degraded by losing 20 per cent. of its metal. A bill for 100*l*. in both cases, is equal not to 100 times 10 guilders, but 100 times 8 guilders. The reason is, that the bill will in England buy only as much of the metal as is contained in 100 times 8 guilders. It will exchange, therefore, of course, only for a bill of 800 guilders.

The facts may be expressed in the form of a general rule. The value of a bill drawn upon any country is equal, when it arrives, to all the precious metal which the money for which it is drawn can purchase in the market: a bill for 100*l*., for example, is equal to all the metal which it can purchase, whether it is the same quantity which would be purchased by 100*l*. sterling, or less. To whatever amount the portion which it can purchase is less than what could be purchased by 100*l*. of the coins, the paper money is degraded below what would be the value of the coins, if they circulated in its stead. The exchange, therefore, against any country, can never exceed the amount of two sums; First, the difference between the value of the degraded and the undegraded currency, or that between

the nominal amount of the currency, and the quantity
of the precious metal which it can purchase ; secondly,
the expense of sending the metal, when purchased.
It thus appears, how perfectly unfounded is the
opinion of those (and some political economists of
great eminence are included in the number) who
conceive that the real, not merely the nominal, exchange, may exceed the expense of transmitting the
precious metals. They say, that when, by some
particular cause, a great absorption of the precious
metals has taken place, creating a scarcity in consequence of which goods must be sent from the country
where it is scarce, to bring it back from the countries
where it abounds, bills, drawn by the country in
which it is scarce, upon the countries where it abounds,
may bear a premium, equal to the cost of sending
goods which may fetch in the foreign market the
value of the bill ; and this, in certain cases, may
greatly exceed the cost of sending the precious
metals.

If the facts are traced, the answer will be seen to
be conclusive.

When the exchange between two countries (call
them A and B) is at par, it is implied, that the exports and imports of both are equal: that each receives from the other as much as it sends.   In this
case the goods which A sends to B must be so much
cheaper in A than they can be made in B, that they

can there be sold with all the addition required on account of the cost of carriage: in like manner the goods which B sends to A must be so much cheaper in B, that the cost of carriage is covered by the price which they fetch in A. This cost of carriage, it is obvious, does not affect the exchange, any more than an item in the cost of production.

Next, let us observe what happens, when the state of the exchange is disturbed. Let us suppose that a demand is suddenly created in A, for the means of making payments in B, greatly beyond the value of the former exportations. The demand for bills on B is consequently increased beyond the supply, and the price rises. The question is, what is the limit to that rise in the price of bills? At first it is evident the rise of price is limited to the cost of sending the precious metal. As the metal, however, departs, the value of it rises. If the currency is paper, and its value stationary, the gold will rise, and rise equally, both in currency and commodities. The final question, then, is, what is the limit to the rise in the value of gold?

Before the premium on the bills commenced, goods in A were so cheap, that a portion of them could be sent to B, and sold, with all the addition of the cost of carriage, and of course with the ordinary profits of stock. The whole of the premium on the bills,

O

therefore, is an addition to the ordinary profits of stock.

If A be taken for England, and B for the continent of Europe, the case will be, that English goods, when the interchange is at par, go abroad, and are sold at a price which includes both profits and cost of carriage; when the premium on bills rises only so high as to equal the cost of sending bullion, it is to that extent an additional profit on the sending of goods.

It is evident that, in proportion as this premium should rise, it would not only enhance the motive to increase the exportation of the goods which could be exported with a profit before the rise of the bills, but that it would render many other kinds of goods exportable, which before could not be exported. Thus, when the exchange was at par, there were certain kinds of goods in England, which, after paying cost of carriage, could be sold abroad with a profit; there were certain other kinds which, on account of their high price in England, could not be thus exported; some might thus be 1 per cent. too high to be exported, others 2 per cent. too high, others 3 per cent., and so on. It is obvious that a premium of 1 per cent. on bills would enable the first kind to be exported; a premium of 2 per cent. would enable the second; and a premium of 10 per cent. would enable two or three kinds to be exported, which could not have been exported before. As the counter operation would be of the same kind and the same power, viz. to prevent the importation of foreign goods into England, exportation would be exceedingly increased, importation nearly prevented. The two operations together would be so powerful, that any great deviation from the real par of exchange could never be of long duration. A deviation equal to the cost of sending the precious metal, permanent circumstances might render permanent. If England, for example, sent every year a large amount of the precious metal to India, and received it from Hamburgh, the exchange would be to the extent of the cost of sending the metals, permanently favourable with Hamburgh, unfavourable with India.

If bills of exchange were always drawn for so much weight of gold, the case would be simple. Suppose a bill in London drawn upon Paris for 100 ounces of gold, no man would pay for that bill more gold beyond the 100 ounces than the cost of sending the 100 ounces. He might purchase the 100 ounces at one time with 390*l.* of currency, at another with 410*l.* of currency, but that would be entirely owing to changes in the relative value of the currency and the gold. These changes, it is said, may in certain circumstances, take place from a rise in the value of the gold, the currency remaining of the same value. This implies that gold can become more valuable in one country than in the neighbouring countries; in England, for example, than on the Conti-

nent.   But this it cannot do without increasing the
exports in England, and diminishing, almost to
nothing, the imports.   Suppose the rise in the value
of gold to be 1 per cent., 2 per cent., or to amount to
10 per cent.; at this last rate the goods which could
be sent abroad with the ordinary profit, could be now
sent abroad with 10 per cent. more than the ordinary
profit, while all the other kinds of goods, those
1 per cent., those 2 per cent., those 3 per cent., 4 per
cent. 5 per cent., and so on, too dear to have been
sent before, would now all be sent; at the same time
that the counter operation would be equally strong
to prevent foreign goods from being imported.   These
are the necessary effects of a high value of gold in
one country as compared with other countries; and
they are evidently such as to render it impossible that
a high value of the precious metal in one country,
compared with the neighbouring countries, can ever
in a state of freedom be of long duration.

SECTION XVII.

BOUNTIES AND PROHIBITIONS.

Under this title I include all encouragements and discouragements, of whatsoever sort, the object of which is, to make more or less of production or exchange to flow in certain channels, than would go into them of its own accord.

The argument, on this subject, I trust, will be clear and conclusive, without a multiplicity of words.

If it should appear, that production and exchange fall into the most profitable channels, when they are left free to themselves; it will necessarily follow that, as often as they are diverted from those channels, by external interpositions of any sort, so often the industry of the country is made to employ itself less advantageously.

That production and exchange do, when left to themselves, fall into the most profitable channels, is clear by a very short demonstration.

The cases of production and of exchange require to be considered separately; for, in the case of production, there is hardly any difference of opinion. If a country had no commercial intercourse with other countries, and employed the whole of its productive powers exclusively for the supply of its own consumption, nothing could be more obviously absurd, than to give premiums for the production of one set of commodities, and oppose obstructions of any sort to the production of another; I mean, in the view of Political Economy, or, on account of production : for if any country opposes obstructions to certain commodities, as spirituous liquors, because the use of them is hurtful; this regards morality, and has, for its end, to regulate not production, but consumption. Wherever it is not intended to limit consumption, it seems admitted, even in practice, that the demand will always regulate the supply, in the manner in which the benefit of the community is best consulted. The most stupid governments have not thought of giving a premium for the making of shoes, or imposing a preventive tax upon the production of stockings, in order to enrich the country by making a greater quantity of shoes, and a less quantity of stockings. With a view to the internal supply, it seems to be understood that just as many shoes, and just as many stockings, should be made, as there is a demand for. If a different policy were pursued; if a premium were bestowed upon the production of shoes, a tax or other burthen imposed upon the production of stockings, the effect would only be, that shoes would be afforded to the people cheaper, and stockings dearer, than they otherwise would be : that the people would be better supplied with shoes, worse supplied with stockings, than they would have been, if things had been left to their natural course, that is, if the people had been left to consult freely their own convenience; in other words, if the greatest quantity of benefit, from their labour, had been allowed to be obtained.

All that regulation of industry, therefore, the object of which has been, to increase the quantity of one sort of commodities, lessen the quantity of another, has been directed to the purpose of regulating the exchange of commodities with foreign countries; of increasing, or diminishing, most commonly diminishing, the quantity of certain commodities, which would be received from abroad.

Now it is certain, as has been already abundantly proved, that no commodity, which can be made at home, will ever be imported from a foreign country, unless it can be obtained by importation with a smaller quantity of labour, that is, cost, than it could be produced with at home. That it is desirable to have commodities produced with as small a cost of labour as possible seems to be not only certain, but admitted. This is the object of all the improvements that are aimed at in production, by the division and distribution of labour, by refined methods of culture applied to the land, by the invention of more potent and skilful machines. It seems, indeed, to be a self-evident proposition, that whatever the quantity, which a nation possesses of the means of production, the more productive they can possibly be rendered, so much the better; for this is neither more nor less than saying, that to have all the objects we desire, and to have them with little trouble, is good for mankind.

Not only is it certain, that in a state of freedom no commodity, which can be made at home, will ever be imported, unless it can be imported with a less quantity, or cost, of labour than it could be produced with at home; but, whatever is the country from which it can be obtained with the smallest cost of labour, to that recourse will be had for obtaining it; and whatever the commodity, by the exportation of which, it can be obtained with the smallest quantity of home labour, that is the commodity, which will be exported in exchange. This results, so obviously, from the laws of trade, as not to require explanation. It is no more than saying, that the merchants, if left to themselves, will always buy in the cheapest market, and sell in the dearest.

It seems, therefore, to be fully established, that the business of production and exchange, if left to choose its own channels, is sure to choose those, which are most advantageous to the community. It is sure to choose those channels, in which the commodities, which the community desires to obtain, are obtained with the smallest cost. To obtain the commodities, which man desires, and to obtain them with the smallest cost, is the whole of the good which the business of production and exchange, considered simply as such, is calculated to yield. In whatever degree, therefore, the business of production and exchange is forced out of the channels into which it would go of its own accord, to that degree the advantages arising from production and exchange are sacrificed ; or, at any rate, postponed to something else. If there is any case, in which they ought to be postponed to something else, that is a question of politics, and not of political economy.

There is no subject, upon which the policy of the restrictive and prohibitive system has been maintained with greater obstinacy, and with a greater quantity of sophistry, than that of the trade in corn. There can, however, be no doubt, that corn never will be imported, unless when it can be obtained from abroad with a smaller quantity of labour than it can be produced with at home. All the good, therefore, which is obtained from the importation of any commodity, capable of being produced at home, is obtained from the importation of corn. Why should that advantage which, in the case of corn, owing to the diversities of soil and extent of population, is liable to be much greater than in the case of any other commodity, be denied to the community?

The reasons, upon which the advocates for a restriction of the corn trade chiefly support themselves, are two ; neither is of any value.

The first is, That unless the nation derive its corn from its own soil, it may, by the enmity of its neighbours, be deprived of its foreign supply, and reduced to the greatest distress. This argument implies an ignorance both of history, and of principle : Of history, because, in point of fact, those countries which have depended the most upon foreign countries for their supply of corn, have enjoyed beyond all other countries, the advantage of a steady and invariable market for grain : Of principle, because it follows unavoidably, if what, in one country is a favourable, is in other countries an unfavourable season, that obtaining a great part of its supply from various countries is the best security a nation can have against the extensive and distressing fluctuations which the variety of seasons is calculated to produce. Nor is the policy involved in this argument better than the political economy. It sacrifices a real good, to escape the chance of a chimerical evil : an evil so much the less to be apprehended, that the country, from which another derives its supply of corn, is scarcely less dependant upon that other country for a vent to its produce, than the purchasing country is for its supply. It will not be pretended, that a glut of corn, in any country, from the loss of a great market, with that declension of price, that ruin of the farmers, and that depression of rents, which are its unavoidable consequences, is an immaterial evil.

The second reason, upon which the advocates of the corn monopoly support themselves, is, That, if the merchants and manufacturers enjoy in certain cases the monopoly of the home supply, the farmers and landlords are subject to injustice, when a similar monopoly is not bostowed upon them. In the first place, it may be observed, that, if this argument is good for the growers of corn, it is good for every other species of producers whatsoever ; if, because a tax is imposed upon the importation of woollens, a tax ought to be imposed upon the importation of corn, a tax ought also to be imposed upon the importation of every thing, which the country can produce; the country ought, in short, to have no foreign commerce, except in those articles alone, which it has not the means of producing.

The argument moreover supposes, that an extra-ordinary gain is obtained by the manufacturer, in consequence of his supposed protection ; and that a correspondent evil is sustained by the corn grower, unless he is favoured by a similar tax. The ignorance of principle is peculiarly visible in those suppositions, in neither of which is there a shadow of truth.

The man who embarks his capital in the woollen, or any other manufacture, with the produce of which that of the foreign manufacturers is not allowed to come into competition, does not, on that account, derive a greater profit from his capital. His profit is no greater than that of the man whose capital is embarked in trades open to the competition of all the world. All that happens is, that a greater number of capitalists find employment in that branch of manufacture; that a portion, in short, of the capitalists of the country employ themselves in producing that particular species of manufacture, who would otherwise be employed in producing some other species, probably in producing something for the foreign market, with which that commodity, if imported from the foreign manufacturer, might be bought.

As the man who has embarked his capital in the trade, which is called protected, derives no additional profit from the protection; so the grower of corn sustains not any peculiar loss or inconvenience. Nothing, therefore, can be conceived more groundless than his demand of a compensation on that account. The market for corn is not diminished because a tax is laid upon the importation of woollens; nor would that market be enlarged if the tax were taken off.

His business, therefore, is not in the least degree affected by it.

It would be inconsistent with the plan of a work, confined to the exposition of general principles, to lay open all the fallacies, which lurk in the arguments for restraining the trade in corn. One or two, however, of the sources of deception, cannot be left altogether unnoticed.

The landlord endeavours to represent his own case, and that of the manufacturer, as perfectly similar; though, in the circumstances which concern this argument, they are not only different, but opposite. The landlord also endeavours to mix up his own case with that of the farmer; and upon the success of that endeavour almost all the plausibility of his pretensions depends. That no pretensions are more unfounded, may be seen by a very short process of reasoning. The farmer, as a producer, requires, like every other producer, that all his outgoings be returned to him, with the due profit upon the capital which he employs. The surplus, which the land yields, over and above this return and profit, is what he pays to his landlord; and his interest is not affected by the quantity of that surplus, whether it be great or small. His interest, however, is very much affected by wages; because, in proportion as wages are low, his profits, like all other profits, are high. Wages cannot be low, if corn is dear. The interest, therefore, the permanent interest, of the class of farmers, consists, in having corn cheap. This or that individual in the class may, that is, during the currency of a lease, have an interest in high prices; and the reason of the exception shows the truth of the general rule. The individual, who, during the currency of a lease, has an interest in high prices, is, by his lease, converted, to a certain extent, into a receiver of rent. During the continuance of his lease, if prices rise, he gets, not only his due return of profits as a farmer, but something more, namely, a portion of what is truly rent, and which, but for his lease, would have gone to the landlord.

This, then, is the grand distinction. The receivers of rent are benefited by a high price of corn; the producers of corn, as such are not benefited by it, but the reverse. The case of the farmer corresponds with that of the manufacturer, not with that of the landlord. The farmer is a producer and capitalist; the manufacturer is a producer and capitalist; and they have both received all that belongs to them, when their capital is replaced with its profits. The landlord is not a producer, nor a capitalist. He is the owner of certain productive powers in the soil; and all which the soil produces belongs to him, after paying the capital which is necessary to put those productive powers in operation. It thus appears that the case of the landlord is peculiar; that a high price of corn is profitable to him, because, the higher the price, the smaller a portion of the produce will suffice to replace, with its profits, the capital of the farmer; and all the rest belongs to himself. To the farmer, however, and to all the rest of the community, it is an evil, both as it tends to diminish profits, and as it enhances the charge to consumers.

SECTION XVIII.

COLONIES.

AMONG the expedients which have been made use of, to force into particular channels a greater quantity of the means of production, than would have flowed into them of their own accord; colonies are a subject of sufficient importance to require a particular consideration.

The only point of colonial policy, which it is here necessary to consider, is that of trade with the colonies. And the question is, whether any peculiar advantage may be derived from it.

With respect to colonies, as with respect to foreign countries, the proposition will, doubtless, be admitted, that, whatever advantage is derived from trading with them, consists in what is received from them, not in what is sent; because that, if not followed by a return, would be altogether loss.

The return from them is either money or commodities. The reader is by this time fully aware that a country derives no advantage from receiving money, more than from receiving any other species of commodity. It is also plain that where the colony has not mines of the precious metal, it cannot, under the monopoly of the mother country, have money, or any thing else, beside its own productions, to send.

It is needless to consider the case of free trade with a colony, because that falls under the case of trade with any foreign country.

The monopoly, which a mother country may reserve to herself, of the trade with her colonies, is of two sorts.

First of all, she may trade with her colonies, by means of an exclusive company. In this case, the colony has no purchaser, to whom she is allowed to sell any thing, but the exclusive company; and no other seller, from whom she is allowed to buy any thing. The company, therefore, can make her buy, as dear as it pleases, the goods which the mother country sends to her, and sell, as cheap as it pleases, the goods which she sends to the mother country. In other words, the colony may, in these circumstances, be obliged to give for the produce of a certain quantity of the labour of the mother country, a much greater quantity of goods than the mother country could obtain, with the same quantity, from any other country, or from the colony in a state of freedom.

The cases of a trade in these circumstances are

P

two : the first, where the colony receives from the
mother country, luxuries, comforts : the other, where
she receives necessaries; either the necessaries of
life, or the necessaries of industry, as iron, &c.

In that case, in which the colony receives luxuries
and comforts only from the mother country, there is
a limit to the degree in which the mother country is
enabled to profit by the labour of the colony. The
colony may decline receiving such luxuries or comforts, if obliged to sacrifice for them too great a
quantity of the produce of her labour, and may
think it better to employ that great proportion of her
labour, in providing such luxuries and comforts as she
herself is capable of producing.

If, however, the colony is dependant for necessaries upon the mother country, the exclusive company
exercises over the colony a power altogether des-
potic. It may compel her to give the whole produce
of her labour, for no more of the necessaries in question, than what is just sufficient to enable the population of the colony to live. If it is the necessaries
of life, which the colony receives, the conclusion is
obvious. If it is commodities, such as iron, and instruments of iron, without which her labour cannot
be productively employed, the result is precisely the
same. She may be made to pay for these articles so
much of the whole produce of her labour, that nothing but what is necessary to keep the population

alive may remain.   It would be the interest of the mother country, not to lessen the population; because, with the population, the produce would be lessened, and hence the quantity of commodities which the mother country could receive.

Instead, however, of trading with her colonies by means of an exclusive company, the mother country may leave the trade open to all her own merchants, only prohibiting the colony from trading with the merchants of any other country.   In this case, the competition of the merchants in the mother country reduces the price of all the articles received by the colony, as low as they can be afforded—in other words, as low as in the mother country itself, allowance being made for the expense of carrying them.   If it be said that the colonies afford a market; I reply, that the capital, which supplies commodities for that market, would still prepare commodities, if the colonies were annihilated; and those commodities would still find consumers.   The labour and capital of a country cannot prepare more than the country will be willing to consume.   Every individual has a desire to consume, either productively or unproductively, whatever he receives.   Every country, therefore, contains within itself a market for all that it can produce.   This will be made still more evident, when the subject of consumption, the cause and measure of markets, comes under consideration.   There is, therefore, no advantage whatsoever derived, under freedom of competition, from that part of the trade with a colony which consists in supplying it with goods, since no more is gained by it, than such ordinary profits of stock as would have been gained if no such trade had existed. It is nevertheless true that the colony may lose by such a traffic, if the goods, which she is thus compelled to purchase of the mother country, might have been purchased cheaper in other countries.

If there be any peculiar advantage, therefore, to the mother country, it must be derived from the cheapness of the goods, with which the colony supplies her. It is evident, that if the quantity of goods, sugar, for example, which the colony sends to the mother country, is so great as to glut the mother country; that is to supply its demand beyond the measure of other countries, and make the price of them in the mother country lower than it is in other countries, the mother country profits by compelling the colony to bring its goods exclusively to her market, since she would have to pay for them as high as other countries, if the people of the colony were at liberty to sell wherever they could obtain the greatest price.

This advantage, if drawn by the mother country, would be drawn at the expense of the colony. In free trade, both parties gain. In the advantage produced by forcing, whatever is gained by the one party is lost by the other. The mother country, in compelling the colony to sell goods cheaper to her than she might sell them to other countries, merely imposes upon her a tribute; not direct, indeed, but not the less real because it is disguised.

If any advantage is derived from restraining, any otherwise than by an exclusive company, the trade with the colonies, it must consist in forcing the colonies to sell to none but the mother country, not in forcing them to buy from none but the mother country. A great improvement, therefore, in colonial policy would be, to throw open the supply of the colonies, permitting them to purchase the goods which they want, wherever they could find the most favourable market, only restraining them in the sale of their goods: allowing them to buy wherever they pleased, permitting them to sell to none but the mother country.

It is at the same time to be observed, that if the merchants of the mother country have freedom to export the goods which are derived from the colonies, the price of these goods will be raised in their own country to the level of the price in other countries. The competition of the merchants will, also, raise the price of the goods to a correspondent height in the colonies; and thus the benefit to the mother country is lost.

Treaties of commerce are sometimes concluded, for the purpose of limiting the freedom of trade. One country can be limited to another in but two ways; either in its purchases, or its sales. Suppose that Great Britain binds some other country to purchase certain commodities exclusively from her; Great Britain can derive no advantage from such a treaty. The competition of her merchants will make them sell those commodities as cheap to the merchants of that country, as to their own countrymen. Their stock is not more profitably employed than it would be if no such trade existed. There are cases in which a country may gain by binding another country to *sell* to none but itself. If one country is bound to sell no commodities whatsoever, except to another particular country; this is the same case, exactly, with that of a colony bound to sell to none but the mother country. As no free country, however, is likely to bind itself to sell none of its commodities except to one other, this is not a case which we need to regard as practicable or real.

One country may bind itself to sell exclusively to another particular country, not all the articles it has for foreign sale, but only some of them.

These may be articles which yield nothing, even in a state of freedom, but the ordinary profits of stock; as cloth, hardware, hats, &c.: or they may be articles which yield something over and above the ordinary profits of stock; as corn, wine, minerals, &c. which are the source of rent.

One country can derive no advantage from compelling another to sell to it, exclusively, articles of the first sort. If the price which the favoured country pays for the goods is not sufficient to afford the ordinary profits of stock, they will not be produced. If the price which it pays is sufficient to afford the ordinary profits of stock, it would, at that price, obtain the goods, without any treaty of restriction.

The case is different, where the goods yield something, as rent, or the profits of a monopoly, over and above the profits of stock. The quantity which may be sent in this case to the favoured country, may sink there the price of the restricted commodity lower than it is in the neighbouring countries; and lower than the restricted country would, if not under restriction, be enabled to sell it in those countries. To this extent, and to this only, can one country benefit, by confining the trade of another to itself. The restriction may operate to a diminution of the profits of a monopolized commodity, or a diminution of rent.

There is one mode of presenting this subject, which is apt to puzzle a mind not accustomed to trace the intricacies of this science.

Suppose two countries, A and B, of which A is bound by treaty, or otherwise, to receive all its shoes from B, and to sell to B all its sugars: Suppose, also, that A could, if left at liberty, obtain its shoes 50 per cent. cheaper from some other country; in that case, it may for a moment appear, that B obtains the sugars which it buys of A, with 50 per cent. less of its own labour, than it would if A were allowed to purchase where it pleased.

If B paid for the supposed sugars in shoes, it would, no doubt, pay 50 per cent. more in the case of a free trade.

But if there were any other article with which it could purchase those sugars, and which it could afford as cheap as any other country, it would lose nothing in the case of a free trade; it would purchase the same quantity of sugar with the produce of the same quantity of labour as before; only, that produce would be, not shoes, but some other article.

That there would be articles which B could afford as cheap as any other country, is certain, because otherwise it could have no foreign trade.

It may be said, however, that though B might have articles which it could sell as cheap as other countries, they might not be in demand in the country which produced the sugars. But if shoes only were in demand in the colonies, those other articles could purchase shoes where they were cheapest; and thus obtain the same quantity of sugar, in the free, as in the restricted state of the trade.

CHAPTER IV.

CONSUMPTION.

OF the four sets of operations, Production, Distribution, Exchange, and Consumption, which constitute the subject of Political Economy, the first three are means. No man produces for the sake of producing, and nothing farther. Distribution, in the same manner, is not performed for the sake of distribution. Things are distributed, as also exchanged, to some end.

That end is Consumption. Things are produced that they may be consumed; and distribution and exchange are only the intermediate operations for bringing the things, which have been produced, into the hands of those who are to consume them.

SECTION I.

OF PRODUCTIVE AND UNPRODUCTIVE CONSUMPTION.

OF Consumption, there are two species; the distinctive properties of which it is of great importance to comprehend.

These are, 1st, Productive Consumption; 2dly, Unproductive Consumption.

1. That production may take place, a certain expenditure is required. It is necessary, that the labourer should be maintained; that he should be provided with the proper instruments of his labour, and with the materials of the commodity which it is his business to produce.

What is thus expended, for the sake of something to be produced, is said to be consumed productively.

In productive consumption, three classes of things are included. The first is, the necessaries of the labourer, under which term are included all that his wages enable him to consume, whether these confine him to what is required for the preservation of existence, or afford him something for enjoyment. The second class of things consumed for production is machinery; including tools of all sorts, the buildings necessary for the productive operations, and even the cattle. The third is the materials of which the commodity to be produced must be formed, or from which it must be derived. Such is the seed from which the corn must be produced, the flax or wool of which the linen or woollen cloth must be formed, the drugs with which it must be dyed, or the coals which must be consumed in any of the necessary operations.

Of these three classes of things, it is only the second, the consumption of which is not completed in the course of the productive operations. The machinery and buildings, employed in production, may last for several years; the necessaries, however, of the labourer, and the materials, either primary or secondary, of the commodity to be produced, are all completely consumed. Even of the durable machinery, the wear and tear amount to a partial consumption.

2. Thus it is, that men consume for the sake of production. They also consume, however, without producing, and without any view to production. The wages which a man affords to a ploughman, are given for the sake of production; the wages which he gives to his footman and his groom, are not given for the sake of production. The flax which the manufac-

turer purchases, and converts into linen, he consumes productively; the wine which he purchases, and uses at his table, he consumes unproductively. These instances are sufficient to illustrate what is meant, when we speak of unproductive consumption. All consumption, which does not take place to the end that an income or revenue may be derived from it, is unproductive consumption.

From this explanation, it follows, that productive consumption is itself a means; it is a means to production. Unproductive consumption, on the other hand, is not a means. This species of consumption is the end. This, or the enjoyment which is involved in it, is the good which constituted the motive to all the operations by which it was preceded.

From this explanation, it also follows, that, by productive consumption, nothing is lost : no diminution is made of the property, either of the individual, or of the community ; for if one thing is destroyed, another is by that means produced. The case is totally different with unproductive consumption. Whatever is unproductively consumed, is lost. Whatever is consumed in this manner, is a diminution of the property, both of the individual and of the community ; because, in consequence of this consumption, nothing whatever is produced. The commodity perishes in the using, and all that is derived is the good, the pleasure, the satisfaction, which the using of it yields.

That which is productively consumed is **always** capital. This is a property of productive consumption, which deserves to be particularly remarked. A man commences the manufacture of cloth with a certain capital. Part of this capital he allots for the payment of wages; another part he lays out in machinery; and with what remains he purchases the raw material of his cloth, and the other articles, the use of which is required, in preparing it for the market. It thus appears, that the whole of every capital undergoes the productive consumption. It is equally obvious that whatever is consumed productively becomes capital; for if the manufacturer of cloth, whose capital we have seen to be productively consumed, should save a portion of his profits, and employ it in the different kinds of productive consumption required in his business, it would perform exactly the functions performed by his capital, and would, in truth, be an addition to that capital.

The whole of what the productive powers of the country have brought into existence, in the course of a year, is called the gross annual produce. Of this the greater part is required to replace the capital which has been consumed; to restore to the capitalist what he has laid out in the wages of his labourers and the purchase of his materials, and to remunerate him for the wear and tear of his machinery. What remain of the gross produce, after replacing the capital which has been consumed, is called the net produce; and is always distributed, either as profits of stock, or as rent.

This net produce is the fund, from which all addition to the national capital is commonly made. If the net produce is all consumed unproductively, the national capital remains unaltered. It is neither diminished nor increased. If more than the net produce is consumed unproductively, it is taken from the capital; and so far the capital of the nation is reduced. If less than the net produce is unproductively consumed, the surplus is devoted to productive consumption; and the national capital is increased.

Though a very accurate conception may thus be formed of the two species of consumption; and the two species of labour; productive, and unproductive; it is not easy to draw the line precisely between them. Almost all our classifications are liable to this inconvenience. Between things, which differ the most widely, there are almost always orders of things, which approach by insensible gradations. We divide animals into two classes, the rational and irrational: and no two ideas can be more clearly distinguished. Yet beings may be found, of which it would be difficult to say, to which of the two classes they belonged. In like manner, there are consumers, and labourers, who may seem, with some propriety, to be capable of being ranked, either in the productive,

or the unproductive class. Notwithstanding this difficulty, it is absolutely necessary, for the purposes of
human discourse, that classification should be performed, and the line drawn somewhere. This may
be done, with sufficient accuracy both for science and
for practice. It is chiefly necessary that the more
important properties of the objects classified should be
distinctly marked in the definition of the class. It
is not difficult, after this, to make allowance, in practice, for those things which lie, as it were, upon the
confines of two classes; and partake, in some degree,
of the properties of both.

SECTION II.

THAT WHICH IS ANNUALLY PRODUCED IS ANNUALLY CONSUMED.

FROM what we have now ascertained of the nature of production and consumption, it will easily be seen, that the whole of what is annually produced is annually consumed ; or, that what is produced in one year, is consumed in the next.

Every thing, which is produced, belongs to somebody, and is destined by the owners to some use. There are however, but two sorts of use : that for immediate enjoyment, and that for ultimate profit. To use for ultimate profit, is to consume productively. To use for immediate enjoyment, is to consume unproductively.

We have just observed, that what is used for ultimate profit, is laid out, as expeditiously as possible, in wages of labour, machinery, and raw material. This is a fact of primary importance ; and many errors of those who reason loosely in Political Economy, arise from the neglect of it. Whatever is saved from the annual produce, in order to be converted into capital, is necessarily consumed ; because to make it answer the purpose of capital, it must be employed in the payment of wages, in the purchase of raw material to be worked into a finished commodity, or, lastly, in the making of machines, effected in like manner by the payment of wages, and the working up of raw materials. With respect to that part of the annual produce, which is destined for unproductive consumption, there is less frequently any mistake. As it would be attended with a loss to lay in a greater stock of articles of this class than is required, for immediate use, all of them, except a few, of which the quality is improved by their age, are always expeditiously consumed, or put in a course of consumption.

A year is assumed, in political economy, as the period which includes a revolving circle of production and consumption. No period does so exactly. Some articles are produced and consumed in a period much less than a year. In others, the circle is greater than a year. It is necessary, for the ends of discourse, that some period should be assumed as including this circle. The period of a year is the most convenient. It corresponds with one great class of productions, those derived from the cultivation of the ground. And it is easy, when we have obtained forms of expression, which correspond accurately to this assumtion, to modify them in practice to the case of those commodities, the circle of whose production and consumption is either greater or less than the standard to which our general propositions are conformed.

SECTION III.

THAT CONSUMPTION IS CO-EXTENSIVE WITH PRODUCTION.

IT requires only a few explanations to show, that this is a direct corollary from the proposition established in the preceding section.

A man produces, only because he wishes to possess. If the commodity, which he produces, is the commodity which he desires to possess, he stops when he has produced as much as he desires ; and his supply is exactly proportioned to his demand. The savage, who makes his own bow and arrows, does not make bows and arrows beyond what he wishes to possess.

When a man produces a greater quantity of any commodity than he desires for himself, it can only be on one account ; namely, that he desires some other commodity which he can obtain in exchange for the surplus of what he himself has produced. It seems hardly necessary to offer any thing in support of so necessary a proposition ; it would be inconsistent with the known laws of human nature to suppose, that a man would take the trouble to produce any thing without desiring to have any thing. If he desires one thing, and produces another, it is only because the thing which he desires can be obtained by means of the thing which he produces, and better obtained, than if he had endeavoured to produce it himself.

After labour has been divided and distributed, to any considerable extent, and each producer confines himself to some one commodity or part of a commodity, a small portion only of what he produces is used for his own consumption. The remainder he destines for the purpose of supplying him with all the other commodities which he desires; and when each man confines himself to one commodity and exchanges what he produces for what is produced by other people, it is found that each obtains more of the several things, which he desires, than he would have obtained, had he endeavoured to produce them all for himself.

So far as a man consumes that which he produces, there is, properly speaking, neither supply nor demand. Demand and supply, it is evident, are terms which have reference to exchange; to a buyer and a seller. But in the case of the man who produces for himself, there is no exchange. He neither offers to buy any thing, nor to sell any thing. He has the property; he has produced it; and does not mean to part with it. If we apply, by a sort of metaphor, the terms demand and supply to this case, it is implied, in the very terms of the supposition, that the demand and supply are exactly proportioned to one another. As far then as regards the demand and supply of the market, we may leave that portion of the annual produce, which each of the owners consumes in the shape in which he produces or receives it, altogether out of the question.

In speaking here of demand and supply, it is evident that we speak of aggregates. When we say of any particular nation, at any particular time, that its supply is equal to its demand, we do not mean in any one commodity, or any two commodities. We mean, that the amount of its demand, in all commodities taken together, is equal to the amount of its supply in all commodities taken together. It may very well happen, notwithstanding this equality in the general sum of demands and supplies, that some one commodity or commodities may have been produced in a quantity either above or below the demand for those particular commodities.

Two things are necessary to constitute a demand. These are, 1st, a wish for the commodity; 2dly, an equivalent to give for it. A demand means the will to purchase, and the means of purchasing. If either is wanting, the purchase does not take place. An equivalent is the necessary foundation of all demand. It is in vain that a man wishes for commodities, if he has nothing to give for them. The equivalent which a man brings is the instrument of demand. The extent of his demand is measured by the extent of his equivalent. The demand and the equivalent are convertible terms, and the one may be substituted for the other. The equivalent may be called the demand, and the demand the equivalent.

We have already seen, that every man, who produces, has a wish for other commodities, than those which he has produced, to the extent of all that he brings to market. And it is evident, that whatever a man has produced, and does not wish to keep for his own consumption, is a stock which he may give in exchange for other commodities. His will, therefore, to purchase, and his means of purchasing, in other words, his demand, is exactly equal to the amount of what he has produced and does not mean to consume.

But each man contributes to the general supply the whole of what he has produced and does not mean to consume. In whatever shape any part of the annual produce has come into his hands, if he proposes to consume no part of it himself, he wishes to dispose of the whole; and the whole, therefore, becomes matter of supply: if he consumes a part, he wishes to dispose of all the rest, and all the rest becomes matter of supply.

As every man's demand, therefore, is equal to that part of the annual produce, or of the property generally, which he has to dispose of, and each man's supply is exactly the same thing, the supply and demand of every individual are of necessity equal.

Demand and supply are terms related in a peculiar manner. A commodity which is supplied, is always, at the same time, a commodity which is the instrument of demand. A commodity which is the instrument of demand, is always, at the same time, a commodity added to the stock of supply. Every commodity is always, at one and the same time, matter of demand, and matter of supply. Of two men who perform an exchange, the one does not come with only a supply, the other with only a demand; each of them comes with both a demand and a supply. The supply, which he brings, is the instrument of his demand; and his demand and supply are of course exactly equal to one another.

But if the demand and supply of every individual are always equal to one another, the demand and supply of all the individuals in the nation, taken aggregately, must be equal. Whatever, therefore, be the amount of the annual produce, it never can exceed the amount of the annual demand. The whole of the annual produce is divided into a number of shares, equal to that of the people to whom it is distributed. The whole of the demand is equal to as much of the whole of the shares as the owners do not keep for their own consumption. But the whole of the shares is equal to the whole of the produce. The demonstration, therefore, is complete.

How complete soever the demonstration may appear to be, that the demand of a nation must always be equal to its supply, and that it never can be without a market sufficiently enlarged for the whole of its produce, this proposition is seldom well understood, and is sometimes expressly contradicted.

The objection is raised upon this foundation, that commodities are often found to be too abundant for demand.

The matter of fact is not disputed. It will easily, however, be seen, that it affects not the certainty of the proposition which it is brought to oppugn.

Though it be undeniable, that the demand, which every man brings, is equal to the supply, which he brings, he may not find in the market the sort of purchaser, which he wants. No man may have come desiring that sort of commodity, of which he has to dispose. It is not the less necessarily true, that he came with a demand equal to his supply; for he wanted something in return for the goods which he brought. It makes no difference to say, that perhaps he only wanted money; for money is itself goods; and, besides, no man wants money but in order to lay it out, either in articles of productive, or articles of unproductive consumption.

Every man having a demand and a supply, both equal; if any commodity be in greater quantity than the demand, some other commodity must be in less.

If every man has a demand and supply both equal, the demand and supply in the aggregate are always equal. Suppose, that of these two equal quantities, demand and supply, the one is divided into a certain number of parts, and the other into as many parts, all equal; and that these parts correspond exactly with one another; that as many parts of the demand as are for corn, just so many parts of the supply are of corn; as many of the one as are for cloth, so many of the other are of cloth, and so on: it is evident, in this case, that there will be no glut of any thing whether the amount of the annual produce be great or small. Let us next suppose, that this exact adaptation to one another of the parts of demand and supply is disturbed; let us suppose that, the demand for cloth remaining the same, the supply of it is considerably increased: there will of course be a glut of cloth, because there has been no increase of demand. But to the very same amount there must of necessity be a deficiency of other things; for the additional quantity of cloth, which has been made, could be made by one means only, by withdrawing capital from the production of other commodities, and thereby lessening the quantity produced. But if the quantity of any commodity is diminished, a demand equal to the greater quantity remaining, the quantity of that commodity is defective. It is, therefore, impossible, that there should ever be in any country a commodity or commodities in quantity greater than the demand, without there being, to an equal amount, some other commodity or commodities in quantity less than the demand.

The effects, which are produced, in practice, by the want of adaptation in the parts of demand and supply, are familiar. The commodity, which happens to be in superabundance, declines in price; the commodity, which is defective in quantity, rises. This is the fluctuation of the market, which every body sufficiently understands. The lowness of the price, in the article which is superabundant, soon removes, by the diminution of profits, a portion of capital from that line of production : The highness of price, in the article which is scarce, invites a quantity of capital to that branch of production, till profits are equalized, that is, till the demand and supply are adapted to one another.

The strongest case, which could be put, in favour of the supposition that produce may increase faster than consumption, would undoubtedly be that, in which, every man consuming nothing but necessaries, all the rest of the annual produce should be saved. This is, indeed, an impossible case, because it is inconsistent with the laws of human nature. The consequences of it, however, are capable of being traced; and they serve to throw light upon the argument, by which the constant equality has been demonstrated of produce and demand.

In such a case, what came to every man's share of the annual produce, bating his own consumption of necessaries, would be devoted to production. All production would of course be directed to raw produce and a few of the coarser manufactures; because these are the articles for which alone there would be any demand. As every man's share of the annual produce, bating his own consumption would be laid out for the sake of production, it would be laid out in the articles subservient to the production of raw produce and the coarser manufactures. But these articles are precisely raw produce and a few of the coarser manufactures themselves. Every man's demand, therefore, would consist wholly in these articles; but the whole of the supply would consist also in the same articles. And it has been proved, that the aggregate demand and aggregate supply are equal of necessity; because the whole of the annual produce, bating the portion consumed by the shareholders, is brought as the instrument of demand; and the whole of the annual produce, with the same abatement, is brought as supply.

It appears, therefore, by accumulated proof, that production can never be too rapid for demand. Production is the cause, and the sole cause, of demand. It never furnishes supply, without furnishing demand, both at the same time, and both to an equal extent.

It has been objected, that, for the validity of the argument it is necessary to suppose, " that new tastes and new wants spring up with the new capital." A single reflection will, I think, make it clear that the taste, and wants, in question, are essentially and necessarily implied in the very existence of the capital.

The new capital is all to be laid out in the purchase of something, according to the plans of the owner. It is of infinite importance to observe, that every creation of capital is the creation of a demand. It is surprising that this material point is so frequently overlooked. It seems to be little less than self evident, and if admitted, it carries in itself an answer to every argument that has been, or that can be adduced, in favour of the glut.

What is it that we mean, when we say the demand of a nation, speaking of the aggregate, and including a definite circle of production and consumption, such as that of a year? Do we, or can we, mean any thing but its power of purchasing? And what is its power of purchasing? Of course, the goods which come to market. What, on the other hand, is it we mean, when, speaking in like manner aggregately, and including the same circle, we say the supply of the nation? Do we, or can we mean any thing, but the goods which come to market? The conclusion is too obvious to need to be drawn.

What produces the confusion of ideas, which so often occurs in the consideration of this subject, is the glut, which may, and does take place, of particular commodities. Does it follow from this, that there can be a glut of commodities in the aggregate, when it is necessarily true that there cannot be an aggregate supply without an equal aggregate demand, equal both in quantity and in value?

To the argument, which shows that to the same degree, in which one or more commodities may be in such abundance as exceeds the demand, some other commodities must fall short of the demand, it has been replied, that the commodities which are supplied in superabundance fall in value, that this involves all the evil of the glut, and is therefore a reply to the whole of the argument which denies its existence.

This is a reply in words only. What is maintained in my argument is, that there can be no glut of commodities in the aggregate, though there may be in particular instances. The answer made to me is, that there may be a glut in particular instances.

In the very words of the pretended reply, the certainty of the disputed fact is admitted. The value, it is said, of the goods, which are in the state of superabundance, falls. If this is not a play upon the word, it implies the very thing which it is brought to dispute, that whenever one set of goods is supplied above the demand, another is supplied below the demand.

What is it that is necessarily meant, when we say that the supply and the demand are accommodated to one another? It is this : that goods which have been produced by a certain quantity of labour, exchange for goods which have been produced by an equal quantity of labour. Let this proposition be duly attended to, and all the rest is clear.

Thus, if a pair of shoes is produced with an equal quantity of labour as a hat, so long as a hat exchanges for a pair of shoes, so long the supply and demand are accommodated to one another. If it should so happen that shoes fell in value, as compared with hats, which is the same thing as hats rising in value compared with shoes, this would imply that more shoes had been brought to market, as compared with hats. Shoes would then be in more than the due abundance. Why? Because in them the produce of a certain quantity of labour would not exchange for the produce of an equal quantity. But for the very same reason hats would be in less than the due abundance, because the produce of a certain quantity of labour in them would exchange for the produce of more than an equal quantity in shoes.

What is true of any one instance is true of any number of instances. It is therefore universally true, that, as the aggregate demand and aggregate supply of a nation never can be unequal to one another, so there never can be a superabundant supply in particular instances, and hence a fall in exchangeable value below the cost of production, without a corresponding deficiency of supply, and hence a rise in exchangeable value, beyond cost of production, in other instances. The doctrine of the glut, therefore, seems to be disproved by reasoning perfectly conclusive.

Let us recapitulate the points. A glut, as it is supposed in this doctrine, namely an excess of production in the aggregate, can take place only by a continued increase of production. Let us imagine that we have just come to the supposed point, when, the supply being full, any additional production will be so much of glut. The additional production takes place, and comes to market. What is the consequence? This new product seeks an equivalent. That is to say, it is a new demand. How then is it possible to say that every new supply is a glut, when a new demand is created equal to it? It is obviously nugatory to say, that this new supply may not find purchasers, or the new demand may not find the commodities to which it is directed; for this is only to say that in particular instances there may, from miscalculation, be superabundance or defect. The natural effects, in such a case, may be easily traced, and they afford decisive evidence. The commodities, of which the additional production consists, may be naturally supposed to consist of some of the sorts which are previously in the market. By supposition, the goods previously in the market were accommodated to one another, no species being either in defective, or superabundant supply. The addition which is made to some sorts of these goods, by the new production, would render them superabundant, if there was not a new demand created. These goods would fall in exchangeable value as compared with others, others would rise in exchangeable value as compared with them. But there is a new demand created; for the owner of the new produce, as he has come into the market to sell goods of some kinds, so he has come to buy goods of some other kinds. As the supply, which he brought, of certain kinds of goods tended to reduce their value, so the demand, which he brings, for other kinds tends to increase their value. The result is, that now there are certain kinds of goods, which it is less profitable than usual to produce; others, which it is more profitable than usual to produce: and this is an inequality, which tends immediately to correct itself. This is the mode, in which every addition is made to the productions of

R

a country, and it is a mode, which is evidently the same at every stage of the progress, from the greatest defect, to the greatest excess, of national riches. It commonly, of course, happens, that the man, who brings into the market an addition of produce, endeavours to bring it in goods that are in defective supply, and to purchase goods that are in superabundant supply; and the state of the market generally enables him to do so: so that an addition of produce brought into the market may just as often remedy a glut as be in any degree the cause of it.

The doctrine of Mr. Malthus, on the subject of the glut, seems, at last, to amount to this: that if saving were to go on at a certain rate, capital would increase faster than population; and that if capital did so increase, wages would become very high, and profits would sustain a corresponding depression. But this, if it were all allowed, does not prove the existence of a glut; it only proves another thing, namely, that there would be high wages and low profits. Whether such an increase of capital, scarcely coming within the range even of a rational supposition, would be a good thing or an evil thing, it would infallibly produce its own remedy, as the power of capital to increase is diminished with the diminution of profits.

Mr. Malthus further says, that the high wages thus produced would generate idleness in the class of labourers. The prediction may be disputed; but, allowed to be correct, what is its import? If, wages continuing the same, less work is done, this is higher pay for an equal quantity of labour; it is therefore the same thing as a rise of wages. It would merely accelerate that diminution of profits, which must in time retard and finally stop the increase of capital, in consequence of which wages would naturally fall. This, therefore, is not a different objection from the former; it is precisely the same objection, only in a different form.

Mr. Malthus, thus, totally failing to prove a glut, even from a continued increase of capital greater than the greatest increase of population, substitutes, for arguments to prove that effect, arguments to prove certain other effects.

Hs says, that were the annual produce thus to go on increasing, its *value* would be diminished. But this is merely a play upon the word. He says, I call the value of a commodity the number of days' wages it is equal to. If then wages are more than doubled, though you double the amount of your commodities, and have twice as much of every thing, yet you will have less value. An arbitrary change, however, in the meaning of a word proves nothing. The facts, and their relations, remain the same, whatever Mr. Malthus, or I, may choose to call them. The facts still are merely these, that society would have the supposed amount of commodities, and all its benefits, and that wages would be very high.

Mr. Malthus further says, that this rapid increase of capital would tend to diminish production. That on which the increase of production depends, is the increase of its two instruments, capital and labourers. By the very supposition which Mr. Malthus himself has made, and on which he is reasoning, both of these instruments are increasing at their most rapid possible rate. It seems therefore a most extraordinary supposition, that production should not be increasing at its most rapid possible rate.

If it be true, as Mr. Malthus supposes, that the high wages supposed would diminish labour, it will be true that less work will be done, and less production effected, than if every man worked more. Let us suppose that the diminution of labour goes on gradually, as wages increase, till at last each man does only half as much work as before, what then is the consequence ? Merely this, that if population is going on at its greatest possible rate, doubling itself in twenty years, there will not be a greater increase of production from labour, than there would be if it doubled itself only in forty years, and each man performed twice as much work. This would still be a more rapid rate than that at which capital increases, except in some very rare and extraordinary circumstances. But, if labour were so very dear, and capital so abundant, the consequence would be, that as little as possible of production would be performed by man's labour, as much as possible by machinery and cattle. Ingenuity would be racked to find the means of superseding the most costly instrument. Machines would be multiplied and improved without end; and a much greater proportion of the annual produce would be the result of capital, a much less the result of immediate labour. The diminution of production would not therefore be nearly in proportion to the diminution of each man's labour.

The supposed effects therefore are really of no importance, otherwise it might still be questioned how far the inference is warranted, that high wages tend to diminish industry. Experience seems to be very full on the opposite side. Where wages are excessively low, as in Ireland, there is no industry; where excessively high, as in the American United States, there is the greatest. What does Mr. Malthus himself mean by the stimulus which he says is given to industry by an enlargement of the market?

SECTION IV.

IN WHAT MANNER GOVERNMENT CONSUMES.

ALL consumption is either by individuals, or by the government. Having treated of the consumption of individuals, it only remains that we treat of that which has government for its cause.

Although the consumption by government, as far as really necessary, is of the highest importance, it is not, unless very indirectly, subservient to production. That which is consumed by government, instead of being consumed as capital, and replaced by a produce, is consumed, and produces nothing. This consumption is, indeed, the cause of that protection, under which all production has taken place; but if other things were not consumed in a way different from that in which things are consumed by government, there would be no produce. These are reasons for placing the expenditure of government under the head of unproductive consumption.

The revenue of government must be derived from rent, from profits of stock, or from wages of labour.

It is, indeed, possible for government to consume part of the capital of the country. This, however, it can only do for one year, or for a few years. Each year in which it consumes any portion of the capital, it so far reduces the annual produce ; and, if it continues, it must desolate the country. This, therefore, cannot be regarded as a permanent source of revenue.

If the revenue of government must always be derived from one or more of three sources ; rent, profits, wages ; the only questions requiring an answer, are ; in what manner, and in what proportion, should it be taken from each ?

The direct method is that which most obviously suggests itself. I shall, therefore, first, consider what seems to be most important in the direct mode of deriving a revenue to government from rent. profits, and wages ; and, secondly, I shall consider the more remarkable of the expedients which have been employed for deriving it from them indirectly.

SECTION V.

TAXES ON RENT.

It is sufficiently obvious, that the share of the rent of land, which may be taken to defray the expenses of the government, does not affect the industry of the country. The cultivation of the land depends upon the capitalist; to whom the appropriate motive is furnished, when he receives the ordinary profits of stock. To him it is a matter of perfect indifference; whether he pays the surplus, in the shape of rent, to an individual proprietor; or, in that of revenue, to a government collector.

In Europe, at one period, the greater part of, at least, the ordinary expenses of the sovereign was defrayed by land, which he held as a proprietor; while the expense of his military operations was chiefly defrayed by his barons, to whom a property in certain portions of the land had been granted on that express condition. In those times, the whole expense of the government, with some trifling exception, was, therefore, defrayed from the rent of land.

In the principal monarchies of Asia, almost the whole expenses of the state have in all ages been defrayed from the rent of land; but in a manner somewhat different. The land was held by the immediate cultivators, generally in small portions, with a perpetual and transferable title; but under an obligation of paying, annually, the government demand; which might be increased at the pleasure of the sovereign; and seldom amounted to less than a full rent.

If a body of people were to migrate into a new country, and land had not yet become private property, there would be this reason for considering the rent of land as a source peculiarly adapted to supply the exigencies of the government; that industry would not, by that means, sustain the smallest repression; and that the expense of the government would be defrayed without imposing any burden upon any individual. The owners of capital would enjoy its profits; the class of labourers would enjoy their wages; without any deduction whatsoever; and every man would employ his capital, in the way which was really most advantageous, without any inducement from the mischievous operation of a tax, to remove it from a channel in which it was more, to one in which it would be less productive to the nation. There is, therefore, a peculiar advantage in reserving the rent of land as a fund for supplying the exigencies of the state.

There would be this inconvenience, indeed, even

in a state of things, in which land had not been made private property; that the rent of the land, in a country of a certain extent, and peopled up to a certain degree, would exceed the amount of what government would need to expend. The surplus ought undoubtedly to be distributed among the people, in the way likely to contribute the most to their happiness; and there is no way, perhaps, in which this end can be so well accomplished, as by rendering the land private property. As there is no difficulty, however, in rendering the land private property, with the rent liable for a part of the public burdens; so there seems no difficulty in rendering it private property, with the rent answerable for the whole of the public burdens. It would only in this case require a greater quantity of land to be a property of equal value. Practice would teach its value as accurately, under these, as under present circumstances; and the business of society would, it is evident, proceed without alteration in every other respect.

Where land has, however, been converted into private property, without making rent in a peculiar manner answerable for the public expenses; where it has been bought and sold upon such terms, and the expectations of individuals have been adjusted to that order of things, rent of land could not be taken to supply exclusively the wants of the government, without injustice. It would be partial and unequal taxation; laying the burden of the state upon one set of individuals, and exempting the rest. It is a measure, therefore, never to be thought of by any government, which would regulate its proceedings by the principles of justice.

That rent, which is bought and sold, however; that rent, upon which the expectations of individuals are founded, and which, therefore, ought to be exempt from any peculiar tax, is the present rent; or at most the present, with the reasonable prospect of improvement. Beyond this, no man's speculations, either in making a purchase, or in making provision for a family, are entitled to extend. Suppose, now, that, in these circumstances, it were in the power of the legislature, by an act of its own, all other things remaining the same, to double that portion of the produce of the land which is strictly and properly rent: there would be no reason, in point of justice, why the legislature should not, and great reason, in point of expediency, why it should, avail itself of this, its own power, in behalf of the state; should devote as much as might be requisite of this new fund to defray the expenses of the government, and exempt the people. No injury would be done to the original land-owner. His rent, such as he had enjoyed it, and to a great degree such even as he had expected to enjoy it, would remain the same. A great advantage would at the same time accrue to every individual in the community, by exemption from those contributions for the expense of the government, to which he would otherwise have had to submit.

The legislature may, without any straining of language, be said to possess that power, which I have now spoken of only as a fiction. By all those measures which increase the amount of population and the demand for food, the legislature does as certainly increase the net produce of the land, as if it had the power of doing so by a miraculous act. That it does so by a gradual progress in the real, would do so by an immediate operation in the imaginary case, makes no difference with regard to the result. The original rent, which belonged to the owner, that upon which he regulated his purchase, if he did purchase, and on which alone, if he had a family to provide for, his arrangements in their favour were to be framed, is easily distinguishable from any addition capable of being made to the net produce of the land, whether it be made by a slow or a sudden process. If an addition made by the sudden process might, without injustice to the owner, be appropriated to the purposes of the state, no reason can be assigned why an addition by the slow process might not be so appropriated.

It is certain, that, as population increases, and as capital is applied with less and less productive power to the land, a greater and a greater share of the whole of the net produce of the country accrues as rent, while the profits of stock proportionally decrease. This continual increase, arising from the circumstances of the community, and from nothing in which the landholders themselves have any peculiar share, does seem a fund no less peculiarly fitted for appropriation to the purposes of the state, than the whole of the rent in a country where land had never been appropriated. While the original rent of the landholder, that upon which alone all his arrangements, with respect both to himself, and his family, must be framed, is secured from any peculiar burden, he can have no reason to complain, should a new source of income, which cost him nothing, be appropriated to the service of the state; and if so, it evidently makes no difference to the merits of the case, whether this new source is found upon the land, or found any where else.

If we assume with Mr. M'Culloch,* that the whole of what the land can ever yield, is conferred, in the case supposed, on the owner of the land, by the previous legislation, there is an end of the question; for it is impossible for any one to express a more decided opinion, than I entertain, against partial taxation; against imposing burthens upon the property of any one class more than upon the property of an-

* See a very masterly article on Taxation in the Supplement to the Encyc. Britan. p. 617.

other class. The real question is, whether any thing, beyond a certain amount of annual benefit, namely, what is at present derived, with such increase as can be rationally anticipated within the number of years' purchase for which the land would sell, can, in a really equitable, excluding a merely technical, mode of considering the subject, be regarded as the property of the land-owner. The considerations, which I have adduced, seem to me to establish, that no point of utility would be violated by such a restriction of the meaning of the term as I have proposed.

I utterly disallow the parallelism of the case of capital, which Mr. M'Culloch has adduced; as if because increased profits of stock ought not to be exclusively taxed, therefore the rent, which accrues in the manner above supposed, could not be justly appropriated to the service of the state. Nobody is more aware of the fundamental differences between profits of stock and rent of land than Mr. M'Culloch : it is, therefore, the more surprising that he should have founded his argument on an agreement between them, which does not exist.

Only a few lines before, in the same passage, he recognizes such a distinction between rent and profits, as in my opinion is fatal to his argument. " The circumstance," he says, " of rent unavoidably rising in the progress of society, inclines us to think that it would be good policy for the governments of countries, such as the United States, which are possessed of large tracts of fertile and unappropriated land, to retain the property of this land in their own hands :" that is, in other words, to reserve the rent for the service of the state. The case of profits is not only different, but the reverse. Instead of rising, in the progress of society, they decrease. Land exists by the gift of nature; capital is the product of human industry. Land is originally not the property of any man; capital always is. The profits of stock must be secured to the owner to afford a motive for its preservation and augmentation. For the preservation of the land, or the augmentation of its produce, it is not of the least importance to whom the rent is consigned. Profits are, in reality, the fund, out of which rent is always taken; and every increase of rent, in the progress of society, is a deduction from profits, in other words, may be regarded as a tax upon profits, not for the benefit of the state, but that of the landlords.

SECTION VI.

A TAX ON PROFITS.

A DIRECT tax on profits of stock offers no question of any difficulty. It would fall entirely upon the owners of capital, and could not be shifted upon any other portion of the community.

As all capitalists would be affected equally, there would be no motive to the man, engaged in any one species of production, to remove his capital to any other. If he paid a certain portion of his profits, derived from the business in which he was already engaged, he would pay an equal portion, derived from any other business to which he could resort. There would not, therefore, in consequence of such a tax, be any shifting of capital from one species of employment to another. The same quantity of every species of goods would be produced, if there was the same demand for them. That there would, on the whole, be the same aggregate of demand, is also immediately apparent. The same capital is supposed to be employed in the business of production; and if part of what accrued to the capitalist was taken from him, lessening to that extent his means of purchasing, it would be transferred to the government, whose power of purchasing would be thence to the same degree increased.

There would, therefore, be the same demand, and the same supply: there would also be the same quantity of money, and the same rapidity of circulation; and therefore the value of money would remain the same as before.

SECTION VII.

A TAX ON WAGES.

IF wages are already at the lowest point, to which they can be reduced; that is, just sufficient to keep up the number of labourers, and no more; the state of wages which seems to have been contemplated, by Mr. Ricardo, throughout his disquisitions on political economy, and which the tendency of population to increase faster than capital, undoubtedly leads us to regard as the natural state; no tax can fall upon the labourer; and if any tax is imposed upon wages, it is easy to trace in what way it must produce a corresponding rise of wages. If wages are as low as is consistent with the preservation of the number of labourers, take any thing away from those wages, and the number of labourers must be reduced. The reduction of the number of labourers must be followed by a rise of wages, and this process must continue till wages rise sufficiently high to be consistent with the preservation of the number of labourers; in other words, just as high as they were before the tax was imposed.

If wages are not at this lowest rate; if they are

sufficiently high to afford the labourers something more than what is necessary to keep up their numbers, something which may be retrenched without a diminution of their numbers, they may, to this extent, be made subject to taxation.

Wages, like the price of any other commodity, rise or fall, in proportion as the demand for labour rises or falls, compared with the supply.

When wages are so low as barely to keep up the number of labourers, wages must rise to the amount of any tax imposed upon them, because there is a continued diminution of the supply of labourers till this rise is effected.

In the case of wages above this level, there is no necessary reduction of the number of labourers in consequence of a tax imposed upon wages. There is no alteration, therefore, in the state of supply. From this it follows, that if there is not an increase of demand for labourers, in consequence of such a tax, there can be no rise of wages; and if there be no rise of wages, the tax must fall upon the labourers. The solution, therefore, of the question, whether a tax upon wages falls upon the labourer, depends upon the inquiry, whether there is, or is not, such increase of demand.

An increase of demand for labour can arise from

two causes only; either from an increase of capital,
the fund destined for the employment of labour; or
a difference in the proportions between the demand
for the produce of fixed capital and that of immediate
labour.

The first of these causes needs no illustration.
The operation of the second we proceed to trace. As
the demand of a nation consists of a great number of
demands of a great number of individuals, the case of
one individual will exemplify the whole.

Suppose a man with a certain income; to determine our ideas, let us call it 1000*l.* per annum; this
is his demand. Let us suppose it divided into two
portions, the one of which constitutes his demand
for the produce of fixed capital; the other his demand for that of immediate labour : and let us suppose that these proportions are different at two different times. We have to examine what are the consequences.

Let us suppose that, first, he spends 500*l.* of this
income on the produce of fixed capital ; 500*l.* on that
of immediate labour.

In the first case he purchases commodities only ; in
the second case he purchases either commodities or
services, but gives the same employment to labour
whether he purchases the one or the other   If a

man makes a basket in a day, for which you pay him a shilling, or weeds in your garden a day at a shilling's wages; in both cases the demand you furnish for labour is precisely the same. The 500*l.* expended in the produce of immediate labour, is a demand for that number of labourers, whose wages for a year amount to 500*l.*; say for 1000 labourers.

If the commodities, made with fixed capital, on which he spends the other 500*l.*, are made purely with fixed capital; an imaginary case, but which we may suppose, for the sake of illustration; this portion of his income presents no demand for labour at all. The price of the commodities which are thus purchased is wholly made up of profits. It is the result of labour formerly expended, and, with the portion of labour now in the market it has nothing to do.

Suppose that of this 500*l.* one half is turned, by a change in the taste of the owner, from the purchase of commodities, the produce of fixed capital, to the purchase of the produce of immediate labour. Two things happen: a demand is created for 250*l.* worth of mere labour: a demand is annihilated for 250*l.* worth of the produce of fixed capital; that is to say, as much of the capital of the country as yielded 250*l.* of profits, becomes useless. This is entirely distinct from a fall in the rate of profits. Such a fall may or may not accompany such a change in the two species of demand. This is a loss of capital. Capital, to this extent, ceasing to be employed, ceasing to be needed, is, to any useful purpose, destroyed. Along with it there is destroyed a productive power to the extent of 250*l.* per annum. This is not compensated by any new production; for by the supposition the number of labourers is not increased. Every labourer that is employed, under the new application of this 250*l.* of the supposed income, would have been employed if the new application had not taken place, if the capital had not been destroyed.

Under the new distribution of the 1000*l.* income, as much is awarded to the class of labourers, as is taken from the class of capitalists. 250*l.* were formerly awarded as profits, which are now awarded as wages. So far, there is no absolute loss, as much being gained by one, as lost by another. The loss arises from this, that, while no new labour is brought into employment, and no addition is made to the productive powers of labour, nor of course to its produce, a portion of capital is thrown out of employment, its productive powers are lost, and the annual produce of the country is diminished.

This case is reversed when machinery is invented which performs the work of immediate labour. Let us make the same supposition of the extreme cases as before; that the machine invented performs the functions of labour without the aid of labour, that the produce is purely the result of capital. Let us suppose a capital of 10,000*l*.; wholly, in the first instance, employed in the payment of wages. Let us suppose that this 10,000*l*. is afterwards expended in making a machine which produces the same commodity, and the same quantity of it. In this case the whole of the labourers who received the 10,000*l*. of wages, are deprived of their old employment. The consequence is, not that they are thrown out of employment, but that they increase the supply of labour in the market and reduce wages. The labourers, in this case, do not necessarily cease to produce; they produce just as much as before. The whole of the produce of the machine, therefore, is a new production, an addition to the former amount of the annual produce.

Compare now the two cases; the case where the demand for the produce of fixed capital is diminished, and that for immediate labour is increased; and the case where the demand for the produce of fixed capital is increased, and that for immediate labour is diminished. In the first there is a rise of wages, and a diminution of profits, and so far there is compensation : but there is besides this a defalcation of production to the extent of the productive powers of all the capital superseded; and this is a dead loss. In the second case, there is a fall of wages, and a rise of profits, so far again there is compensation; but in this case there is an increase of production to the extent of the productive powers of the whole of the fixed capital created. This is a new fund for the employment of labour, and as far as it goes, prevents the fall of wages.

Having thus illustrated the only case in which an increase of demand for labour can take place, without an increase in the amount of capital, which in the case before us is not supposed, we are prepared to see where an increase of demand for labour, in consequence of a tax upon wages, can, and where it cannot, exempt the labourer from the tax.

The effect of a tax upon wages, when wages are so high as to be capable of being affected by a tax, is, to transfer a certain power of commanding the produce of labour and capital from the class of labourers to the government. With the amount of the tax, before it was taken from the labourers, they presented a demand for so much of the operations of fixed capital, so much of those of immediate labour. Where the same amount is transferred to the government, the government presents in like manner a demand for so much of the operations of fixed capital, so much of those of immediate labour. If the proportions of the demand for the produce of fixed capital and immediate labour were the same in both cases, there would be no alteration in the demand for labour, in consequence of the tax, and the whole of it would fall upon the labourers. If the government presented a greater demand for the produce of immediate labour, less for that of fixed capital, than was presented by the labourers, there would so far be an increase of demand for labour, and a rise of wages, which would so far be a compensation to the labourer for the tax, at the expense, however, of profits, and with an uncompensated loss to the extent of all the produce which the superseded capital would have yielded.

Properly speaking, however, this rise of wages is not an effect of the tax upon wages. It is the effect of a very different cause; of a supposed peculiarity in the nature of the government expenditure. When we are talking, therefore, of the effect of a tax upon wages, in increasing or diminishing the demand for labour, this extraneous circumstance, which may or may not be concomitant, ought to be left out of the account. The only essential effect of a tax upon wages is to take so much from the labourer, just as a tax upon profits takes so much from the capitalist, a tax upon rent takes so much from the landlord.

It is further essential to this question to observe, that the effect of the government expenditure in raising wages, by furnishing a greater demand for immediate labour, less for the produce of fixed capital, would take place equally if the tax were levied upon profits, or upon rent. If this is the effect of the expenditure of government, upon whatever source of income the tax is levied, to lay the tax upon wages is only to prevent the labourer from reaping the benefit of that rise of wages, the full benefit of which he would otherwise enjoy. In this sense, therefore, also, and, when this is included, all are included, it is evident that the tax really falls upon the labourer.

The argument may be shortly stated thus. Before the tax, a certain demand existed for labour; arising, in part from the funds of the landlord, in part from those of the capitalist, and in part from those of the labourer. After the tax the two former remain the same. But the demand arising from the funds of the labourer is diminished. If this loss of demand were not compensated, the labourer would sustain two evils in consequence of the tax. He would pay the tax; and his wages would fall. The second of these evils he does not sustain, because the diminution of demand on the part of the labourers is compensated. The increase of demand on the part of government is exactly equal to the diminution of the demand on the part of the labourers. This prevents wages from falling, but it does no more. It yields nothing in compensation for the tax.

SECTION VIII.

DIRECT TAXES WHICH ARE DESTINED TO FALL EQUALLY UPON ALL SOURCES OF INCOME.

ASSESSED taxes, poll taxes, and income taxes, are of this description. After what has been said, it is not difficult to see upon whom, in each instance, the burden of them falls.

In as far as they are paid by the man, whose income is derived from rent, or the man whose income is derived from profits of stock, the burden of them is borne by these classes. No additional demand arises from the tax; and, therefore, neither can landlords raise their rents, nor capitalists the price of their commodities.

In respect to the labourer, the result is different in different cases. If his wages are already at their lowest rate, no portion of such tax can fall upon him. His wages will rise, and throw his share upon the capitalist. If the wages of the labourer are sufficiently high, he will sustain his share of the burthen.

The effect of these taxes upon prices may be easily ascertained. A tax upon rent would produce no alteration in the price of any thing. Rent is the effect of price; and the effect cannot operate upon the cause. A tax upon profits would alter prices, only as a tax upon wages alters them.

Of the tax upon wages, there are two cases; that in which it raises wages, and that in which it does not raise them. In the case in which it does not raise them it will hardly be supposed that any alteration of prices should ensue. The capital of the country is not supposed to undergo any alteration, nor, of course, the quantity of produce. With respect to the demand, a portion of the power of purchasing, which belonged to the labourers, is taken from them : but the whole of what is taken from them is transferred to the government. Government may send abroad the amount of the tax. If we suppose, however, that it sends it abroad in goods, it is evident, that no diminution of prices will ensue. And if it sends it abroad in bullion, the case, in the long run, is the same; for as the vacuity which is thus made in the bullion market, is to be supplied, goods must go abroad to purchase it. The exportation of the bullion, if it diminishes the quantity of money, will produce a temporary depression of price. But the same effect would follow from the same cause on any other occasion.

In the case in which wages do rise, it may also be seen, that the capital and produce of the country remain the same, the amount of demand and supply the same, and the value of money the same. The aggregate of prices, therefore, one thing being compensated by another, is the same. That change, indeed, which takes place in the relative value of certain kinds of commodities, as often as wages rise and profits fall, is necessarily produced on this occasion. Those commodities, which are chiefly produced by fixed capital, and where little payment of wages is required, fall in price, as compared with those in producing which immediate labour is the principal instrument, and where little or nothing of fixed capital is required. The compensation, however, is complete; for as much as the one of these two sets of commodities falls in price, the other rises; and the price of both, taken aggregately, or the medium of the two, remains the same as before.

The several species of property, which, in the ordinary and coarse application of language, pass under the name of income, are exceedingly different. This gives occasion to a question, whether it is equitable to levy the same rate of tax upon all incomes. The question, however, in what proportion taxes ought to fall, is rather a question of general policy, than of political economy; which, in regard to taxes, confines itself to two questions: first, on which of the three original shares of the annual produce, rent, wages, or profits, a tax falls : and next, whether it operates unfavourably on production.   As this question, however, is generally introduced into books on political economy, it is proper here to point out the way to its solution.

The grand distinction of incomes, as regards this question, seems to be, the value of them.   All property may, with trifling exceptions, be regarded as income.   But the value of incomes depends upon two circumstances: first, upon what is called their amount, as 100*l.* per annum, or 1000*l.* per annum; secondly, their permanence and certainty.   Thus the value of a man's property is ten times as great, if he has 1000*l.* a year, as if he has 100; but that only if the permanence and security are equal; for if 100*l.* a year is secure for ever, while 1000*l.* a year is only to endure for a few years, the 100*l.* a year will be the more valuable property of the two.   That, on the occasion of imposing a tax, property is to be estimated, according to one of the elements of its value, and not according to all of them, is a proposition which ought not to be admitted except on very substantial grounds.

Let us suppose, that one man's income is 100*l.*, the rent of land; that another man's income is 500*l.*, the salary of his office, depending not only upon his life and health, but in some degree upon the pleasure of his employers.   The first will be worth 30 years' purchase; the last, in certain circumstances, not worth more than six. The real value of the property of these two men will, in these circumstances, be the same; and upon the principle of equal burthens upon equal property, the tax upon these ought to be the same.

It is true that, if the tax, proportional to the amount, is paid for 30 years upon the 100*l.* and six years upon the 500*l.* the amount of tax will be the same. But this, as a principle of taxation, is liable to this objection; that it excludes from consideration that, to which all consideration should tend, individuals, and their feelings.

There is another point of view in which we must consider the question. The period of enjoyment of the man whose income is 100*l.* in rent, may be as short as that of the man whose income is 500*l.* in salary; the life of the first may not be worth a greater number of years' purchase than the salary of the second.

In this way, undoubtedly, all incomes may be regarded as measured by the life of the individual.

It may also be affirmed, that, in like manner as the income of the man, who draws rent, passes to his descendants; so the income of the man who draws salary, passes to his successors. Strictly speaking, the two species of income are both equally permanent : the rent flows in a permanent stream, through one generation after another, and so does the salary. It would follow, therefore, that if rent were taxed at one rate, salaries at another, there would be two perennial streams of income, taxed in different degrees, the one more, the other less heavily.

This is true, and the only reason for such difference is, the difference of those who succeed to the incomes.   In the case of income derived from land or from capital, the income passes to a man's children, to the persons most dear to him : in the case of salaries, it passes to those, with whom the man has no connexion.   Whether this reason is sufficient, requires to be considered.   There can be no doubt that in regard to feelings, in regard to the happiness of the individuals, it makes a great difference, whether their incomes are to pass to their children at their deaths, or to their successors, in their offices, or their professions. On this score it would seem to be required by the principle of all good legislation, that a corresponding difference should be observed in the imposition of taxes.

This, however, would be a step, it is said, towards the equalizing of fortunes.   It would lessen the incomes of the descendants of the owners of permanent incomes, in order to increase those of the descendants of persons with life incomes.   This is liable to the same objections as raising the scale of taxation, in proportion to the scale of income; taxing commodities, for example, higher to the man of 1000*l*., than to the man of 100*l*. a year. It would lessen the motive to make savings, by lessening the value of great accumulations. It is to be inquired whether this allegation is well founded.

A **tax,** to operate fairly, ought to leave the relative condition of the different classes of contributors the same, after the **tax,** as before it. In regard to the sums required for the service of the state, this is the true principle of distribution.

In the case of incomes of different permanency, what does leave the relative condition the same?

It is quite clear, that the prospect for a man's children is one part of that condition. If a tax so operates upon two classes, as to reduce the condition of the children of the one class lower, as compared with the condition of the children of the other class, than it would otherwise be, it does not leave the relative condition of those two classes the same.

Suppose two men, each of 1000*l*. a year, the one rent, the other salary; the latter worth 15 years' purchase. Suppose that to make a provision for his children, the man with the salary saves one-half; the man with the rent spends all. With respect to expenditure, the man with the salary stands to the other in the relative condition of a man of half the income.

Next let us examine how it is with the children. The annual sum of 500*l*. saved for 15 years, at compound interest, would amount, say, to 10,000*l*. This at 5 per cent. interest, would afford a perpetual income to the children of the man with the salary of 500*l*. a year. The children of the man with the rent would have 1000*l*. In this way, as the father's condition was that of a man with half the income, so is that of the children.

It is perfectly plain, therefore, that if the one is taxed at more than one half the rate of the other, he is taxed too high. The salary we supposed to be worth 15 years' purchase: the rent is worth 30: one half is here also the proportion. It therefore points out the rule. If one income is worth half as many years' purchase as another, it ought to be half as much taxed; if it is worth one-third of as many years' purchase, it ought to be taxed one-third, and so on.

It may be said, that if the class who live upon salaries are loaded with more than their due share of the burthen, the balance will adjust itself; because, the situation having been rendered less desirable, fewer people will go into it, and the salaries will rise. This does not remove the objection. For, first of all, why should legislation disturb the natural proportion, in order that the force of things may restore it? In the next place, the restoration of the equilibrium in this case is a slow operation. It requires a generation to pass away before the diminution of the numbers of those who live upon salaries can raise their condition. A whole generation is therefore sacrificed.

SECTION IX.

TAXES ON COMMODITIES; EITHER SOME PARTI-
CULAR COMMODITIES; OR ALL COMMODITIES
EQUALLY.

TAXES on commodities may either affect some particular kinds, or all commodities equally.

When a tax is laid on any particular commodity, not on others, the commodity rises in price, or exchangeable value; and the dealer or producer is re-imbursed for what he has advanced on account of the tax. If he were not re-imbursed, he would not remain upon a level with others, and would discontinue his trade. As the tax is, in this case, added to the price of the goods, it falls wholly upon the consumers.

When a tax, in proportion to their value, is laid upon all commodities, there is this difference, that no one commodity rises in exchangeable value, or, as compared with another. If one yard of broad cloth was equal in value to four yards of linen, and if a duty of ten per cent. on the value were laid upon each, a yard of cloth would still be equal to four yards of linen.

An *ad valorem* duty upon all commodities would have the effect of raising prices, or their value in relation to money.

The members of the community would come to market, each with the same quantity of money as before.   One-tenth of it, however, as it came into the hands of the producers, would be transferred to the government.   But it would again be immediately laid out in purchases, either by the government itself, or by those to whom the government might dispose of it.   This portion, therefore, would come into the hands of the producers oftener by once, after the tax was imposed, than before.   Before the tax was imposed, it came once into the hands of the producers, from those of the purchasers of goods.   After the tax was imposed, it would come into the hands of the producers in the same manner : but it would go from them to the government, and from the government come back into the hands of the producers a second time.

The producers, in this manner, would receive for their goods, not only the whole ten-tenths of the money of the country, as before ; but they would receive one-tenth twice, where they received it only once before.   This is the same thing exactly as if they had received eleven-tenths, or as if the money of the country had been increased one-tenth.   The purchasing power of the money, therefore, is diminished one-tenth ; in other words, the price of commodities has risen one-tenth.

Upon whom the tax would, in that case, fall, is abundantly obvious. The purchasers would come with the same quantity of money as before. The purchasing power of that money, however, would be reduced one-tenth, and they would be able to command one-tenth less of commodities than before. The tax would, of course, fall upon purchasers.

As this argument has not produced, in some minds whose decisions I highly respect, the same conviction which it has in my own, I will endeavour to render it still more perspicuous, by recurrence to one of the simplest possible cases.

Let us suppose a community of 10 persons, with only two species of commodities, bread, and meat. Let us suppose that 5 of those persons have 5 loaves to dispose of, and that the other 5 have 5 pounds of meat, the value of a loaf the same as that of a pound of meat. Let us suppose that the exchange takes place, as in a more complicated state of things, by the intervention of money; and, as the simplest possible case, let us suppose that the whole of the goods is exchanged against the whole of the money; in other words, that one exchange of the whole of the goods is performed by one operation of the money. If each loaf is worth 10 pence, and each pound of meat the same, it is necessary, under this supposition, that the 5 persons having the 5 loaves of bread should have 50 pence, and the persons having the 5 pounds of meat should have 50 pence.

It is obvious that the persons having the 5 loaves, going to market with 50 pence to buy the 5 pounds of meat, will pay for it at the rate of 10 pence per pound, and that the persons with the meat, going to market for the bread, will pay for it at the rate of 10 pence the loaf. If we suppose that the production of the loaves and the meat is perpetually renewed, it is evident that the same exchanges, at the same money price, may take place for ever. All this, I think, is clear.

Let us then suppose, that government taxes these commodities 10 per cent., and observe attentively what happens. When the first loaf of bread is sold for 10 pence, one penny out of the 10 pence received is paid by the seller to the government, and when one pound of meat is sold, one penny out of the 10 pence received is in like manner paid to the government. By the time that one exchange of all the commodities is effected, one-tenth of the money has been paid to government. With the money, government, as fast as it received it, has come into the market to purchase the same goods. The former purchasers came with all the former quantity, namely, with 100 pence, government came with a tenth more. For the same quantity of goods, therefore, for which 100 pence were paid before, 110 pence have been paid now; it is therefore proved that the price of goods is raised at the rate of the tax. The reason is, that one portion of the money which only performed one operation, in effecting one exchange of the goods, now performs two operations.

The case would be precisely the same, if we supposed the rapidity of circulation to be much greater, and that each piece of money had to perform 10 operations in order to effect one exchange of the whole of the commodities. It is necessary to observe that this is the only correct meaning of the term rapidity of circulation. This is the only meaning in which rapidity of circulation has any effect upon the value of the money. This is strictly, therefore, the sense in which the term is here employed. If we suppose that in order to perform one exchange of the whole of the commodities, the money has to be exchanged 10 times, it is obvious, as before explained, that it exchanges each time for precisely one-tenth of the goods. Let us conceive that the bread and the meat, supposed in the former case, are 10 times as great, the loaves 50, and the pounds of meat 50, the money remaining the same, but performing 10 operations to effect one exchange of the whole. It is very obvious that the effect which we have just explained, as taking place, in consequence of the tax, upon the whole of the goods, when the whole was exchanged by one operation of the money, will now take place upon the one-tenth of the goods which is exchanged by one operation of the money; it will be raised one-tenth in money value; each tenth will be so raised; and therefore by necessary consequence the whole.

SECTION X.

A TAX UPON THE PRODUCE OF THE LAND.

A TAX upon the produce of land, a tax upon corn, for example, would raise the price of corn, as of any other commodity. It would fall by consequence, neither upon the farmer, nor upon the landlord, but upon the consumer. The farmer is situated as any other capitalist, or producer; and we have seen sufficiently in what manner the tax upon commodities is transferred from him that produces to him that consumes.

The landlord is equally exempted. We have already seen that there is a portion of the capital employed upon the land, the return to which is sufficient to yield the ordinary profits of stock, and no more. The price of produce must be sufficient to yield this profit, otherwise the capital would be withdrawn. If a tax is imposed upon produce, and levied upon the cultivator, it follows that the price of produce must rise sufficiently to refund the tax. If the tax is 10 per cent. or any other rate, upon the selling price, corn must rise in value one-tenth, or any other proportion.

In that case it is easy to see, that no part of the tax falls upon the landlord. It is the same as if one-tenth of the produce were paid in kind. In that case, it is evident, that one-tenth less of the produce would come to the landlord; but as it would rise one-tenth in value, his compensation would be complete. His rent, though not the same in point of produce, would be the same in point of value.

If, instead of a money-tax, varying according to price, it were a fixed money-tax upon the bushel, or the quarter, the money-rent of the landlord would still be the same. Suppose the land or capital, which, as explained above, yields no rent, to produce in all two quarters, that which does yield rent to produce six quarters; four quarters, in that case, are the share of the landlord. Suppose the tax per quarter to be 1*l.*; corn must rise 1*l.* per quarter. The farmer, before the imposition of the tax, paid the landlord the price of four quarters; after it, he pays him the price of four quarters, deducting 1*l.* per quarter for what he had paid as tax. But corn has risen 1*l.* per quarter. He, therefore, pays him the same sum as before.

SECTION XI.

A TAX UPON THE PROFITS OF THE FARMER, AND UPON AGRICULTURAL INSTRUMENTS.

IF a tax were imposed upon the profits of the farmer, without being imposed upon the profits of any other class of producers, the following would be its effects.

It would in the first place raise the price of raw produce; because that price is determined by the produce of the capital which pays no rent, and which, if it sustains a tax, must rise like any other taxed commodity, to indemnify the producer.

In consequence of this rise of price, it would increase the rent of the landlords. Suppose that capital is employed on the land in this case under three degrees of productiveness: the most productive portion yielding 10 quarters, the second 8, and the last 6. A landlord who had land cultivated under these circumstances, would receive at the rate of 6 quarters of corn as rent. 4 produced by the first portion, and 2 by the second. Suppose a tax imposed such as to raise the price of corn 5 per cent.: it leaves the 6 quarters of corn, accruing to the landlord, the same as before ; but the value of these 6 quarters is 5 per cent. higher ; the landlord's rent, therefore, is increased 5 per cent.

The difference between this case, and those treated of in the preceding section, is, that the landlord's portion of the produce is not taxed, when the profits of the farmer are taxed.

A tax upon the instruments of agriculture, is the same thing in effect, as a tax upon the profits of the farmer. It raises the value of produce, without affecting the quantity which goes as rent to the landlord. Thus, if a tax is laid upon agricultural horses, it increases the expense of production to the farmer, just as a tax upon coals would increase the cost of production to the iron-founder. For this cost the farmer can only be indemnified by a rise in the price of the produce. The quantities, however, of the corn, the 10, the 8, the 6 quarters, yielded to the different portions of his capital, are not affected. Six quarters of corn are the rent of the landlord, the same as before. Not only, therefore, does the whole of the tax fall upon the consumer, but he is charged with another burthen, the additional rent which is paid to the landlord. The community is taxed, in part for the use of the government, in part for the benefit of the landlords.

SECTION XII.

TITHES AND POOR RATES.

TITHES are a tax upon the produce of the land; a tenth of the produce, perfectly or imperfectly collected.

The operation, therefore, of this tax, has been already ascertained. It raises the price of produce, and falls wholly upon the consumer.

If the poor rate were levied in proportion to profits upon farmers, manufacturers, and merchants, it would be a tax upon profits. If it were levied in proportion to the rent of land, it would be a tax upon the rent of land. If it were levied upon the rent of houses, it would fall upon the inmates, and be a tax upon income. From the mode in which it is levied, it is drawn in part from all these sources. If it falls disproportionately upon the profits of any one class of capitalists, that class receives compensation. If the farmers, as is usually supposed, pay a higher rate for the maintenance of the poor than other producers, this, as far as the excess extends, is the same thing as a separate and additional tax upon them. But if a separate tax is laid upon the farmers, we have already seen that it operates immediately to raise the price of corn sufficiently high to afford them compensation for the tax, and raises the rent of the landlords. It is to them a benefit, not a burthen.

Of all taxes which raise the price of corn, one effect is remarkable. As a certain quantity of corn is necessary to the subsistence of the labourer, his wages must be competent to the purchase of that quantity. They must often, therefore, rise as the price of that quantity rises. But we have already seen, that, in proportion as wages rise, profits fall. A tax upon corn, therefore, operates upon all men as consumers. Upon capitalists it is apt to operate in two ways; it is, first, a tax upon them as consumers; and, secondly, it has often the same effect upon them as a tax upon their profits.

SECTION XIII.

A TAX PER ACRE ON THE LAND.

WE have already considered in what manner a tax, laid upon the land, and proportioned to the rent; in what manner a tax laid upon the land, and proportioned to the produce; and in what manner a tax laid upon the land, and proportioned to the farmer's profits, would operate. The first would be a tax upon the landlord; the second would be a tax upon the consumer, and would not affect the landlord; the third would be a tax upon the consumer, and would benefit the landlord. A tax may also be laid upon the land at so much per acre.

We have seen that there is a portion of capital employed upon the land, the return to which is sufficient to afford the ordinary profits of stock, but nothing more. If any addition is made to the cost of producing, a rise of price must afford compensation. If no addition is made to such cost, price will not be affected.

If a tax is laid, at so much per acre, on land, both cultivated, and uncultivated, no addition will be made to the cost of producing. There are two cases in which portions of capital are employed on the land, without yielding more than the ordinary profits of stock; of course yielding nothing for rent: the one is, where, after two or more doses of capital have been bestowed upon land, each yielding less than the former, a third or a fourth comes to be employed; the other is, where, after land of the second or third degree of fertility has been exhausted, cultivation is forced upon land of a still inferior quality.

It is evident, immediately, that a tax on the acre does not affect the cost of production, when a subsequent dose of capital is employed upon the same land; because the tax is already paid; and it is, therefore, the interest of the farmer to apply a second dose, as soon as the price of produce has risen sufficiently high to afford him a full profit and nothing more.

When capital is applied to new land of inferior quality, upon which the tax was previously paid, the cultivator receives his remuneration the moment produce rises sufficiently high to afford the profits of the stock which the cultivation may require; and no allowance is to be made for a tax which does not depend upon the cultivation.

When the tax is levied only on cultivated land; as

U

capital passes downwards from the more fertile land which has been cultivated before, to the less fertile, which has not been cultivated, the tax likewise descends. The produce to be raised must yield, not only the ordinary profits of stock, but the tax also; such land will not be cultivated till the price of produce has risen sufficiently high to yield that accumulated return. The tax, therefore, is included in the price.

The consequence, with regard to the landlord, is beneficial. Suppose that land of the third degree of fertility is the last to which cultivation has descended; that such land yields at the rate of two quarters per acre, land of the next degree above it at the rate of four quarters, and land of the first degree of fertility six quarters; in this case, it is evident, that two quarters upon each acre affords both the tax, and the remuneration to the farmer. The landlord, therefore, may derive two quarters from the acre of second quality, four quarters from the acre of first. He draws this quantity of produce, in both cases; as well when such a tax is levied, as when it is not levied. But in the case of the tax, the price is raised, and each of his quarters of corn is of greater value. Such a tax would, therefore, raise upon the consumers, not only so much per acre to the government, but a great deal more for the benefit of the landlords.

One effect, however, of this tax would be, to retard

the descent of capital to the inferior species of land. So long as fresh doses of capital, upon the land already in cultivation, were not diminished in productive power, to the whole extent of the tax, below what would be the productive power of capital employed upon the best of the uncultivated land, no capital would be employed upon it, and, during that interval, the cost of corn would be raised to the consumer, and additional rent would go to the landlord, without affording any revenue to the state.

When first imposed, such a tax would have the effect of throwing an inferior species of land out of cultivation, wherever an additional dose of capital, on the better land, would not in productive power fall below that, which had gone to the worse land, to an extent equal to the tax. This would still raise the price of corn, because, by the supposition, the last portion of capital would be less productive than before ; it would also increase the rent of landlords, but not so much as the full operation of the tax.

SECTION XIV.

TAXES UPON THE TRANSFER OF PROPERTY.

TAXES upon the transfer of property are of several kinds; such as stamp duties upon purchase and sale, legacy duties, duties upon the writings required in the conveying of property, and others of the same nature.

In the case of all that property, which is the produce of labour and capital, the tax upon purchase and sale falls upon the purchaser, because the cost of production, including the profits of stock, must be afforded along with the tax.

Taxes upon the transfer of land, which is a source of production, and not the effect of labour and capital, fall upon the seller; because the purchaser considers what benefit he could derive from his capital employed in another way; and if the land will not afford him an equivalent, he will refuse to exchange it for the land.

Legacy duties, and duties upon free gifts, fall, it is evident, upon the receivers.

SECTION XV.

LAW TAXES.

TAXES upon proceedings at law are levied chiefly in the form of stamps, on the different writings employed in the business of judicature; and in that of fees on the several steps and incidents of the judicial procedure.

It is evident enough that they fall upon the suitors. It is equally evident that they are a tax upon the demand for justice.

Justice is demanded in two cases; either that, in which it is a matter of doubt to which of two persons a certain right belongs; or that, in which the right of some person has been violated, and a remedy is required.

There is no peculiar propriety in taxing a man, because he has a right, which, unfortunately for him, is disputed. But there is the greatest of all improprieties in taxing a man, because he has sustained an act of injustice.

It is very evident that all such taxes are a bar in the way of obtaining redress of injury; and just in so far as any thing obstructs the redress of injury, injustice is promoted. A tax upon justice, therefore, is a premium upon injustice.

SECTION XVI.

TAXES ON MONEY, AND THE PRECIOUS METALS.

A TAX upon money cannot be conveniently levied, excepting either upon the occasion of its coinage, or that of the first acquisition of the bullion. It might be levied upon the bullion, either upon its importation from abroad; or, if the mine were within the country, upon its issuing from the mine.

A tax upon coinage is the same thing, in effect, with what has been called a seignorage. It is the paying of something more for the coins, than the quantity of bullion of which they are composed.

The effect of this is evident, when a currency consists entirely of the metals. No man will carry bullion to be coined, unless the metal in the coin is of as much more value than the bullion, as the amount of the tax. The currency, therefore, is raised in value; that is to say, the metal in the state of currency is raised in value, to an amount equal to that of the tax.

This is a tax which possesses the peculiar property of falling upon nobody. It falls not upon the man who carries bullion to be coined, because he carries it only when the coins are equal in value to the tax and bullion together. It falls not upon the persons to whom the coins are paid as the medium of exchange ; because they are of the same value to them as if they contained the whole of the bullion for which they will exchange.

This is a tax, therefore, which ought always to be carried as far as the peculiar limit to which it is subject will admit. The limit to which it is subject, is the inducement to illicit coining. If the tax is raised so high as to pay the coiner for his expenses and the risk of detection, illicit coinage is ensured.

In a country, in which paper circulates along with gold, the paper has a tendency to prevent the effect of a seignorage.

It is the interest of those who issue paper, to maintain in circulation as great a quantity of it as they can. They may go on increasing the quantity, till it becomes the interest of those who hold their notes to bring the notes to them for coins.

It is the interest of those who are the possessors of notes, to carry them to the bank for coins, only when there is a profit by melting. The coins, as coins, are not more valuable than the paper, so long as they circulate, without a premium, along with the paper.

But if the paper has been issued in great quantity, the value of the currency may be so reduced, that the metal in the coins may be of more value as bullion than as coin. Melting for the sake of this profit, is the only check upon the quantity of a paper money convertible into coins at the option of the holder.

It is very obvious, that if coins are issued under a seignorage, with the metal in the coins of greater value than the metal in the state of bullion, the coins can be retained of that value only if the currency is limited in amount. When paper is issued without restriction, that limit is removed. The paper issued increases the quantity of currency, till the metal in the coins is reduced, first to the same value as that in bullion, next to a less value. At that point it becomes the interest of individuals to demand coins at the bank, for the purpose of melting; and then it is the interest of the bank to contract its issues.

A very simple, however, and a very effectual ex- pedient, is capable of being adopted, for preventing this effect of a paper currency. That is an obliga- tion on the bank to pay for its notes, either in coins, or in bullion, at the option of the holder. Suppose that an ounce of gold is coined into 3*l.*, deducting five per cent. for seignorage, and suppose that a bank which issues notes is bound to pay, on demand, not only 3*l.* of coins, but an ounce of bullion, if preferred; it is evident that the bank, in that case, has an interest in preventing the currency from sinking in value. If the currency is so high in value, that 3*l.* of currency is really equal in value to an ounce of bullion, the bank loses nothing by being obliged to give for it an ounce of bullion; if it is so depressed in value that 3*l.* is not worth an ounce of bullion, it does lose. The check upon the issue of paper is thus made to operate earlier.

A tax upon the precious metals, when imported, or extracted from the mines, would, as far as the metals were destined to the ordinary purposes of use or ornament, fall upon the consumers: it would, as far as the metals were used for currency, fall upon nobody.

It would raise the exchangeable value of the metal. But a smaller quantity of a valuable metal is not less convenient as the medium of exchange, than a greater quantity of a less valuable. It would be expedient, therefore, to derive as much as possible from this source. The facility, however, of carrying and concealing a commodity which involves a great value in small dimensions, renders it a source from which much cannot be derived. Under a very moderate duty, illicit importation would be unavoidable.

Though a tax upon the precious metals, as imported, or issued from the mines, would, like all other taxes upon particular commodities, fall ultimately upon the consumer, it would not do so immediately. That which enables the producers, when a tax is laid upon any commodity, to throw the burden upon the consumers, is the power they have of raising the price, by lessening the supply. Of most commodities, the quantity in use is speedily consumed. The annual supply bears, therefore, a great proportion to the quantity in use; and if it is withheld, or only a part of it withheld, the supply becomes so far diminished as greatly to raise the price. The case is different with the precious metals. If the annual supply were wholly withheld, it would, for some time, make no great defalcation from the quantity in use. It would, therefore, have little effect upon prices. During that interval the sellers of the metals would not be indemnified. During that time, more or less of the tax would fall upon them.

The same observation applies to houses, and all other commodities of which the quantity in use is great in proportion to the annual supply.

SECTION XVII.

EFFECTS OF THE TAXATION OF COMMODITIES UPON THE VALUE OF MONEY, AND THE EMPLOYMENT OF CAPITAL.

CAPITAL is most advantageously employed, when no inducement whatsoever is made use of to turn it out of one employment into another. It is most advantageously employed, when it follows that direction which the interest of the owners would give to it of its own accord.

Suppose that broad cloth is in England twenty shillings per yard; that linen, if made at home, would be three shillings per yard: that in Germany, on the contrary, linen is at two shillings per yard; and that broad cloth, if made there, would be twenty-four shillings per yard.

It has been already seen, how, in these circumstances, it would be the interest of England to employ her labour in making broad cloth for Germany, instead of linen for herself; and that of Germany, in making linen for England, instead of broad cloth for herself.

If, in these circumstances, a tax in England were laid upon broad cloth, which raised the price to twenty-four shillings, what would be the consequence?

In the first place, it is evident, that no broad cloth could be exported to Germany.   The price, however, of linen, would still be so low in Germany, that it would be imported into England.   Money, instead of cloth, would go abroad to pay for it. Money, therefore, would become comparatively scarce in England ; and prices would fall.   It would become comparatively abundant in Germany, and prices would rise.   Linen would, therefore, become too dear to be imported into England ; unless in the mean time some other commodity, in consequence of the increasing value of money, became cheap enough in England to allow exportation.   In the first case, England would, by a tax upon her own broad cloth, be deprived of the advantage of obtaining cheap linen from Germany, and would be obliged to produce it for herself.   In the other case, she would be compelled to export, in exchange for the linen, another commodity, which, by the supposition, she produced on less favourable terms than the first.

In this manner it is evident that, by a tax imposed upon broad cloth, the people of England would suffer, not only by paying the tax upon broad cloth, but by being obliged to pay more also for their linen.

The effect of this tax upon prices would be, to raise the money value of broad cloth, and to lower the money value of all other commodities: not to raise, at least permanently, the price of cloth to the whole amount of the tax; because it would send part of the money out of the country: to lower the price of all other commodities, because by this departure of the money, the value of money would be raised.

If, when the tax was imposed upon broad cloth, a drawback of the whole of the duty was allowed upon exportation, there would be no alteration in the trade with Germany; English broad cloth would be sent there, and linen would be imported, on the same terms as before. The people of England would sustain the burden of the tax, and would suffer no other injury. There would be no transit of the precious metals. The price of broad cloth would be raised in England; and the price of all other things would remain as before.

Even if no drawback were allowed, taxes have not a necessary tendency to lessen the quantity of foreign trade. Though England, as in the case already supposed, were hindered, by the tax on broad cloth, from exporting broad cloth; she might soon, by the transit of money, have it in her power to export some other commodity. The reason of this case, it will easily be seen, applies to all other cases. A highly taxed country may possibly export to as great an extent as if she had not been taxed at all. If care, however, has not been taken, and it seldom is taken, to compensate exactly for established duties by countervailing duties and drawbacks, it does not export with the same advantage.

There are two cases, in which the money cost of commodities may be raised by taxation: that in which commodities to any number are taxed one by one, as in the instance, just adduced, of broad cloth; and that in which all commodities are taxed by an *ad valorem* duty. In neither of these cases, it will be seen, has the high price of commodities, in other words, the low purchasing power of money, a necessary tendency to send money out of the country.

In the case adduced above, the broad cloth alone was enhanced in price by the tax. The purchasing power of money was lessened, therefore, only in respect to broad cloth. But money could not go out of the country with any greater advantage to purchase broad cloth; because that commodity, on importation, would have to pay the tax; and there would not be a new distribution of the precious metal, if the tax were drawn back.

Neither would an *ad valorem* duty, though it would raise, in the manner already explained, the price of all commodities, and reduce the purchasing power of money, have a tendency to send money out of the country. Suppose the duty ten per cent.; and the purchasing power of money reduced as much below the level of the surrounding countries. It would be of no avail to the merchant that his money would purchase ten per cent. more of goods abroad, if he were obliged to pay ten per cent. duty upon their importation. It thus appears, that, if drawbacks and countervailing duties are applied upon exportation and importation, the price of commodities in one country may be raised to any extent above their price in the surrounding countries.

THE END.

C. Baldwin Printer,
New Bridge-street, London.

www.ingramcontent.com/pod-product-compliance
Lightning Source LLC
Chambersburg PA
CBHW062036090426
42740CB00016B/2925